St Teres
the Our Father

A Catechism of Prayer

ALOYSIUS REGO OCD

With a Foreword by James McCaffrey OCD

First published 2015 by:

TERESIAN PRESS
Carmelite Priory
Boars Hill
Oxford OX1 5HB
priory@carmelite.org.uk

ISBN 978-0-947916-17-6

A catalogue record for this book is available
from the British Library.

Cover design by Joshua Horgan, Oxford

Typeset and printed by Joshua Horgan, Oxford

For my nephews and nieces:

Adrian, Xavier, Naomi and Natasha
My pride and my joy!

With an Uncle's love

Contents

Foreword

It is a great pleasure for me, during this Centenary Year of Teresa of Avila, to introduce *St Teresa and the Our Father* by Fr Aloysius Rego, OCD, one of our friars from Varroville, New South Wales. In 2009, Teresian Press brought out his excellent introduction to the teachings of St Thérèse of Lisieux, *Holiness For All*, which has been very well received and presents her message with both simplicity and insight.

His latest book is equally helpful and compelling, making accessible to readers, in the clearest way possible, the essential message of the writings of our great Carmelite saint and Doctor of the Church.

St Teresa's discussion of the Our Father, which occupies about half of her work *The Way of Perfection*, is considered a classic commentary on the Lord's Prayer and a mini-spiritual classic in its own right. Devoting several pages to each of the petitions of this great prayer which Jesus gave us, Teresa approaches it with an eye to the spiritual depths contained within it. The notion of 'heaven', for example – as in the words *who art in heaven* – does not apply solely to the afterlife but, as Teresa shows, to the 'little heaven of our soul', where God dwells, and where we live with him already in an intimate exchange, eternal and already begun.

Teresa also recognises that Jesus is indicating for us, in this prayer, what should be the central goal of every Christian: *to do the Father's will*. And she also sees how Jesus is pointing the way to how we might do this: he gives us his *kingdom* here below – his presence with us and in us – and he gives us the Eucharist, *our daily bread* for the needs of each day, which is offered to us this day, every day.

While, at all times, the author has a gift of great clarity in bringing before our eyes the teachings of Teresa's commentary, he perhaps excels in his discussion of the petition *Lead us not into temptation*, where he does justice admirably well to Teresa's perceptive insights – showing us, in this way, *how to discern temptations* in the spiritual life (of which we may not even be aware), and *what remedies we may employ* to overcome them.

Readers might ask: Why do we need a book to tell us what Teresa said, when we can read her for ourselves? While there is, of course, no substitute for reading a saint's works at first hand, it is also true to say that the kernel of Teresa's message is not always immediately clear, not least because of the various avenues she explores, which is a sign of her rich and lively mind. What Fr Aloysius does is to extract the essence of her message, the way one does indeed draw out the kernel from a shell.

Or, to use another image: he provides us, as it were, with a map that shows us the main roads, the turnings-off, and the scenic routes, too, of the journey in prayer that Teresa is sharing with us. To have this book to hand, then, allows us to read, or reread, Teresa's own commentary with ease and understanding – secure in the knowledge that we know where we are going, so that we can understand all the road signs and settle back to enjoy and savour the beauty of the landscape while never losing sight of the goal of our journey to which God is calling us.

Even for those readers who have not yet encountered Teresa's own commentary on the Lord's Prayer, or who pick up this book without any knowledge of the saint who inspired it, *St Teresa and the Our Father* stands alone, in its own right, as a most helpful and inspiring work on the spiritual life. It is written by someone who is a born teacher and who has dedicated his life to prayer. This book is, indeed, a 'catechism of prayer'.

James McCaffrey, OCD
Editor of *Mount Carmel*
& Director of Teresian Press

Feast of Our Lady of Mount Carmel, 2015

Prologue

The Our Father, often known as the 'Lord's Prayer', is *the* Christian prayer *par excellence*. It is the prayer shared by all Christians, disciples of Jesus, irrespective of the Church to which they belong. This is not surprising, given the fact that the Our Father is an evangelical prayer – and the prayer that Jesus himself taught his disciples to pray.

The Our Father is present in the Gospels of St Matthew (Mt 6:9–13) and St Luke (Lk 11:1–4). Matthew's version is the one used in the Church's liturgy and is also the text on which Teresa has based her commentary. In Matthew's Gospel, the Our Father is part of the Sermon on the Mount. As such, it is an integral part of the New Law enshrining the new mode of ethical conduct and of the relationship between human beings and God, and with one another.

In teaching his disciples this prayer, Jesus invites a way of praying that is different from the manner ascribed to the Jewish religious authorities of his day. The scribes and Pharisees thought that by multiplying their words in addressing God, they could compel God to hear their prayers and grant their pleas. In contrast to this mode of prayer, Jesus presents the Our Father as a fundamental pattern of prayer that is most suitable and pleasing to God, and appropriate to our relationship with God.

It is not surprising, then, that many of the Church Fathers, saints and theologians, have meditated upon and written commentaries on this evangelical prayer. St Augustine, for example, in his *Letter to Proba*, expresses the completeness and excellence of the Our Father, and he comments: 'For whatever other words we may say..., if we are praying in the right way, we say nothing that has not already a place in the Lord's prayer. But whoever says anything that cannot be related to this prayer of the gospel, even though he is not praying unlawfully, he is praying in a fleshly, unspiritual manner: and I do not know how that should not be called unlawful, since people reborn of the Spirit ought not to pray otherwise than spiritually.'[1]

St Teresa's commentary on the Our Father, which is now considered a classic, is found in her *Way of Perfection* and is an integral part of this book, which is itself a treatise on prayer. It was written in 1566, at the request of her Carmelite daughters, the Discalced Nuns of the Reform at the convent of San José in Avila: 'The Sisters have urged me so persistently to tell them something about [prayer],' she writes, 'that I have decided to obey them' (WP Prol. 1).[2] The request of the nuns was that of daughters imploring their beloved mother to teach them about prayer.

In this work, consisting of forty-two chapters, Teresa begins by stating the *raison d'être* for her reform of the nuns (chapters 1 and 3) and the importance of poverty (chapter 2). This is followed by fifteen chapters on the three virtues, namely *fraternal charity*, *detachment* and *humility*, and on other essential dispositions which Teresa maintains are the necessary foundations for authentic growth in prayer (chapters 4–18). From chapters 19 to 26, she provides some general reflections and teachings on the nature of prayer, referring to three kinds of prayer – *vocal*, *mental* and *contemplative* – with her main focus being the encouragement of 'mental' prayer. Finally, Teresa offers her commentary on the Our Father (chapters 27–42), which also brings her work to its conclusion.

It must be pointed out here that although Teresa was writing specifically for the nuns of San José, with their requests and needs in mind, and although throughout the text she dialogues directly with her Carmelite daughters, nevertheless this Doctor of the Church has composed a doctrine relevant to all, irrespective of their state in life.[3] Thus, in my book, I will reflect on Teresa's commentary in an *inclusive* manner: as referring not only to her Carmelite daughters, but to ALL of us who listen to her teaching. Accordingly, when Teresa speaks to her nuns, we can also read this as her speaking to *us*.

Those familiar with the writings of Teresa will recognise the experiential nature of her prose. By this I mean that she writes from experience: she draws on her own personal experience and also on the experiences of those with whom she had dealings. Hers, then, is not a dry, detached, intellectual or speculative account of the spiritual life, but rather a lively, engaging, intense, passionate and personal prose. Teresa's writings are a deep sharing of herself with her daughters and with God, such that she frequently breaks into prayer, confession and praise. Given this approach to her writing, Teresa's thought does tend, though, at times to digress. Hence, her thought processes are not always easy to follow, and her readers can sometimes lose the thread of her argument.

This modest work is my own reading of Teresa's commentary on the Our Father, and an attempt to present the essence of her reflections in a focused and coherent manner. I also engage with Teresa's thought by elucidating some of her statements which might be a puzzlement for some of her readers; to do this, I situate such statements, where relevant, within the historical, ecclesial and theological contexts of her times. I have always, though, endeavoured to preserve Teresa's voice where possible.

Finally, I wish to acknowledge the assistance of the following people and express my thanks to them:

– Fr James McCaffrey, OCD, Director of Teresian Press, for inviting and accepting my manuscript for publication, and also for writing the Foreword to this work;

– Joanne Mosley, for her thoroughgoing work in editing my text;

– Clare Murphy, for a careful reading of my manuscript and providing helpful suggestions;

– My parents, George and Celina, and also Sheila Cooper and many unnamed others, for their prayerful support and encouragement.

Aloysius Rego, OCD
Fifth Centenary of the birth of St Teresa, 2015

Chapter 1
A Glance at the Historical Context

The Authorities and the Fear of Mysticism

In Teresa's day, contemplation and mysticism were looked upon with suspicion, distrust and caution by the hierarchy of the Church in Spain. This was the time of the Protestant Reformation. The Catholic Church was in turmoil; it was being challenged and rent apart.

Moreover, in sixteenth-century Spain, especially in Castile, there were burgeoning spiritual movements espousing various forms of mental prayer, and attracting a large number of lay people intent upon a deeper interior life by means of affective prayer, which might be called 'prayer of the heart'. From these movements there emerged two partisan groups: the *recogidos* and the *dejados* (literally, 'the recollected' and 'the abandoned'). Both groups were referred to by the Inquisition as '*Alumbrados*', a name that might be translated as 'The Illumined' (or 'The Illuminists').

While these two groups shared common ideals, there were also certain differences between them.

The first group, the *recogidos*, advocated recollection, by which the soul through detachment from creatures disposes itself to be penetrated by divine action.[4] This group also believed that, without interior love and conviction, the exterior practices of religion were useless. The second group, the *dejados*, promoted self-abandonment.[5] This group emphasised the importance of passivity and interior inspiration, and rejected all forms of exterior devotions and religious practices.[6]

Both groups promoted the importance of mental prayer, contemplation and mystical phenomena. Problems arose, however, in the exaggerations and exclusivism with which these themes were proposed, and in the practical consequences of such distortions. The *dejados* taught that through mental prayer a person was freed from all other religious exercises, such as penance, mortification, the practice of virtue, liturgical prayer and so on. Indeed, passivity and total abandonment to God, they claimed, actually *demanded* the abstention from all interior acts and exterior works, even reflection on the humanity of Christ.[7] All of this, including obedience, was believed to do harm to attaining union with God, which was thought to come through passivity and abandonment.[8] The *dejados* came to be judged by the Inquisition as an unorthodox spiritual movement.

Not surprisingly, during this period in the life of the Church in Spain, there also began to emerge some *lay* mystics – predominantly women. Some of them were false mystics who caused harm by their teaching. Of course, given fallen human nature, these false mystics gained fame and became the focus of attention. This led to the fear of diabolical influence and – importantly for understanding the background to Teresa's life – a repudiation and discouragement of 'mysticism' in general. The Church in Spain responded to this phenomenon by teaching lay people to follow the 'level' and 'safe' paths of asceticism and vocal prayer, and to shun the extraordinary ways of mysticism – especially any phenomena such as locutions, visions and private revelations.[9]

Teresa – An Authority on Prayer

This sceptical ethos, in which, as Teresa remarks, 'there are many persons seemingly terrified by the mere term "mental prayer" or "contemplation"' (WP 24:1), was the very environment in which she founded a monastery of women dedicated to a life of prayer and intimate friendship with God. We have a strong sense of this spiritual background when Teresa writes:

You will hear some persons frequently making objections: 'there are dangers'; 'so-and-so went astray by such means'; 'this other one was deceived'; 'another who prayed a great deal fell away'; 'it's harmful to virtue'; 'it's not for women, for they will be susceptible to illusions'; 'it's better they stick to their sewing'; 'they don't need these delicacies'; 'the Our Father and the Hail Mary are sufficient'. (WP 21:2)

Teresa was in total agreement with this last statement, namely that the Our Father and the Hail Mary are sufficient. But she also contends, quite rightly and pointedly, that if the Our Father is to be prayed well, then it must be joined by *mental* prayer. Of course, what Teresa means by 'mental' prayer is something quite different from that proposed by the *dejados*. And, unlike the Church authorities, Teresa does not fear 'mental' prayer. She says:

> What is this, Christians, that you say mental prayer isn't necessary? Do you understand yourselves? Indeed, I don't think you do, and so you desire that we all be misled. You don't know what mental prayer is, or how vocal prayer should be recited, or what contemplation is, for if you did you wouldn't on the one hand condemn what on the other hand you praise. (WP 22:2)

Here, we see Teresa speaking with authority, and with a broader and more informed understanding of prayer than the *dejados Alumbrados* who disdained vocal prayer, and those Church

20

authorities who feared mental prayer due to misunderstanding its nature. Teresa, on the other hand, offers a strong defence of *mental* prayer, *vocal* prayer and *contemplation*. As we will see, Teresa believed that *vocal prayer should be joined by mental prayer, with the possibility of this leading to contemplation.* Her teaching is both grounded and inspiring, and this makes her a sure and reliable guide on the journey of prayer.

Chapter 2
Three Types of Prayer

The Royal Road to Heaven

Prayer is the principal subject matter of all Teresa's writings. For Teresa, prayer is 'the royal road to heaven' on which everyone is invited to travel (cf. WP 21:1.5). It is also the means towards the fullest possible communion with God in this life.

In her writings, Teresa refers to three different kinds of prayer: *vocal*, *mental* and *contemplative*. Of these, only the first two can be taught and must be worked at; the third, contemplation, cannot be taught but only received and its effects described. A brief exploration of Teresa's understanding of these different kinds of prayer will be helpful for situating her commentary on the Our Father in context.

Vocal Prayer

When it is Prayed Well

By *vocal* prayer, Teresa here is speaking of prayer with words – set prayers such as the Our

Father, the Hail Mary, the divine office and the rosary (cf. WP 22:3; 24:2; 25:3). In sixteenth-century Spain, certain suspect groups, such as the *dejados Alumbrados*, disparaged vocal prayer and advocated passivity in prayer; this caused the Church to promote vocal prayer and to encourage the faithful – especially women – to practise vocal prayer. Ways of praying that involved some degree of passivity, then, were considered suspect by the ecclesiastical authorities and strongly discouraged.

Unlike the *dejados Alumbrados*, who displayed contempt for vocal prayer – claiming it had little or no value, so was an 'inferior' form of prayer – Teresa holds vocal prayer in high esteem, provided it is vocal prayer that is *prayed well*. She maintains that vocal prayer is no obstacle or impediment to the attainment of the highest graces in prayer, including contemplation: 'I tell you,' she writes, 'that it is very possible that while you are reciting the Our Father or some other vocal prayer, the Lord may raise you to perfect contemplation' (WP 25:1). Indeed, Teresa is adamant: 'I know there are many persons who while praying vocally...are raised by God to sublime contemplation without their striving for anything or understanding how' (WP 30:7).[10] She confirms her belief, then, by referring to personal knowledge and experience. She shares with us one example at length:

> I know a person who was never able to pray any way but vocally, and though she was tied to

24

this form of prayer she experienced everything else. And if she didn't recite vocal prayer her mind wandered so much that she couldn't bear it... She spent several hours reciting a certain number of Our Fathers, in memory of the times our Lord shed His blood, as well as a few other vocal prayers. Once she came to me very afflicted because she didn't know how to practise mental prayer nor could she contemplate; she could only pray vocally. I asked her how she was praying, and I saw that though she was tied to the Our Father she experienced pure contemplation and that the Lord was raising her up and joining her with Himself in union. And from her deeds it seemed truly that she was receiving such great favours, for she was living a very good life. So I praised the Lord and envied her for her vocal prayer. (WP 30:7)

An Act of Love

The problem with vocal prayer, however, is that it can tend to become mechanical and mindless. Teresa was well aware of this and was concerned that others should be made aware of it, too. Accordingly, she says that, when praying the Our Father and the Hail Mary, 'it's only right that you should understand what you're saying...so that people won't be able to say of us that we speak and don't understand what we're speaking about

– unless we think it is enough for us to follow the practice in which merely pronouncing the words is sufficient' (WP 24:2). And she urges us:

> What I would like us to do...is refuse to be satisfied with merely pronouncing the words. For when I say, 'I believe', it seems to me right that I should know and understand what I believe. And when I say, 'Our Father', it will be an act of love to understand who this Father of ours is and who the Master is who taught us this prayer. (WP 24:2)

For Teresa, then, vocal prayer is much more than an unthinking recitation of words. Vocal prayer, when prayed well, involves attentiveness to God and intimacy with him. To this end, she sets out to teach us about *mental* prayer, showing us that there is no contradiction between them: 'To recite the Our Father or the Hail Mary or whatever prayer you wish is vocal prayer. But behold what poor music you produce when you do this without mental prayer. Even the words will be poorly pronounced at times' (WP 25:3). For Teresa, vocal prayer without mental prayer is mere babbling.

Mental Prayer

A Prayer of Presence

Teresa explains mental prayer with this direct, even blunt, statement: 'the nature of mental prayer isn't determined by whether or not the mouth is closed' (WP 22:1). Hence, mental prayer is not a technique. And she gives this important explanation:

> If while speaking I thoroughly understand and know that I am speaking with God and I have greater awareness of this than I do of the words I'm saying, mental and vocal prayer are joined. (WP 22:1)

An essential element of mental prayer, then, has to do with awareness of *whom* we are addressing, namely God.

For Teresa, mental prayer does not take any particular form; it is a prayer of *presence*. It may be vocal or silent, as with meditation or reflecting on our relationship with God. What defines mental prayer is an *awareness* of communing with God, as Teresa explains here with no little humour:

> if you are to be speaking, as is right, with so great a Lord, it is good that you consider whom you are speaking with as well as who you are, at least if you want to be polite. How can you call the king 'your highness' or know the ceremonies to be observed in addressing a

highest ranking nobleman if you do not clearly understand what his position is and what yours is? For it is in conformity with these facts that you must show respect, and in conformity with custom – because you also need to know even the customs. If you don't know them, you will be sent away as a simpleton and will fail to negotiate anything. (WP 22:1)

The Three Conditions

Hence, Teresa points out that, for the practice of mental prayer, three conditions must be observed – all of which, we shall see later, are at work in her commentary on the Our Father:

– The first is awareness of *whom* we are speaking with and relating to: that is, God.

– The second is awareness of *who* is the one speaking: that is, oneself.

These first two awarenesses set up a dynamic characterised by the recognition of our status as creatures before God, the Creator. This consciousness of the relationship that exists between God and us gives rise to:

– The third condition: knowing *how* to approach and speak with God.

Reminding us of how to approach God, Teresa advises: 'Yes, indeed, for we must not approach a conversation with a prince as negligently as we do one with a farm worker, or with some poor thing like ourselves for whom any manner of address is all right... Yes, bring yourselves to consider and understand whom you are speaking with, or, as you approach, with whom you are about to speak. In a thousand lives we would never completely understand the way in which this Lord deserves that we speak with Him, for the angels tremble before Him' (WP 22:3.7).

For Teresa, then, if these three elements are present, we are engaging in *mental* prayer – irrespective of whether we are praying with or without words. However, if these elements are *not* present, then we are *not praying at all* – not even vocally. As already pointed out, for Teresa the mere rattle of words, unthinking and inattentive, is not prayer; to suggest otherwise leaves her speechless: 'If, however, others tell you that you are speaking with God while you are reciting the Our Father and at the same time in fact thinking of the world, then I have nothing to say' (WP 22:1). And again: 'You should not be thinking of other things while speaking with God, for doing so amounts to not knowing what mental prayer is' (WP 22:8).

Disposing Ourselves for Contemplation

Fundamentally, for Teresa there is no *real* difference between vocal prayer, prayed with loving presence and attentiveness to God, and mental prayer. So it follows that if we are to practise vocal prayer *well*, it must be *joined with* mental prayer. As Teresa says: 'I tell you that surely I don't know how mental prayer can be separated from vocal prayer if the vocal prayer is to be recited well with an understanding of whom we are speaking to' (WP 24:6).

Mental prayer is the essence of Teresa's teaching: because she believes that it is through the diligent practice of mental prayer that contemplative prayer is likely to be attained. In short, mental prayer is the best means of disposing ourselves for the gift of contemplation. To this end, she strongly encourages us to join mental prayer to our vocal prayer.

Both vocal and mental prayer are *active* forms of prayer: with the help of the Holy Spirit, the prayer is the one who has to do the work to engage with God. By way of contrast, contemplation is a *supernatural* form of prayer, in which God is the principal active agent. As Teresa writes, highlighting the essential differences: 'In these two kinds of prayer [vocal and mental] we can do something ourselves, with the help of God. In the contemplation I now mentioned, we can do nothing; His Majesty is the one who does everything, for it is His work and above our nature' (WP 25:3). However, even in contemplation, the soul is never purely passive but is actively opening itself to receive God's grace. In the words of John of the Cross: 'pure contemplation lies in receiving'.[11]

Contemplation
Under the Action of God

By contemplation, then, Teresa means predominantly passive prayer. This is prayer in which the pray-er is mostly passive. *God*, the Holy Spirit, is, as said, the principal active agent in this prayer. Hence, in contemplation, the Spirit works in us with directness and immediacy. We ourselves are active only insofar as we open ourselves to the Spirit's activity in us.

The graces of contemplation are manifested in many ways. One such experience is given in the following description by Teresa:

> The soul understands that without the noise of words this divine Master is teaching it by suspending its faculties, for if they were to be at work they would do harm rather than bring benefit. They are enjoying without understanding how they are enjoying. The soul is being enkindled in love, and it doesn't understand how it loves. It knows that it enjoys what it loves, but it doesn't know how. It clearly understands that this joy is not a joy the intellect obtains merely through desire. The will is enkindled without understanding how.

But as soon as it can understand something, it sees that this good cannot be merited or gained through all the trials one can suffer on earth. This good is a gift from the Lord of earth and heaven, who, in sum, gives according to who He is. What I have described...is perfect contemplation. (WP 25:2)

Pure Gift

Contemplation, then, is pure *gift*. We cannot attain it by dint of sheer human effort. All we can do is dispose ourselves to receive this gift of God, through perseverance in prayer and virtue. Whether we do in fact receive the grace of contemplation is not dependent on us, but on God. But, as Teresa states, this grace is not necessary for salvation (cf. WP 17:2).

Now, while Teresa acknowledges that we have no right or claim to the gift of contemplation, nevertheless her whole aim is to teach us how to dispose ourselves to receive this gift, so that we may drink 'from the fount of living water' (WP 19:2; cf. Jn 4:14). And to this end, she encourages us in the practice and perseverance of vocal prayer joined with mental prayer.

It is in order to help us to pray vocal prayer well that she shares with us her reflections on the Our Father. We will turn now to consider Teresa's commentary on this evangelical prayer, essential to all Christians.

Chapter 3
Our Father

✝

The very first words of the Lord's Prayer – *Our Father* – lead Teresa to reflect on *whom* we are addressing in prayer. And in pondering these words, she is overwhelmed at the generosity of Jesus. She exclaims: 'O Son of God and my Lord! How is it that You give so much all together in the first words?' (WP 27:2).

A Great Gift

Teresa is astounded that Jesus would grant us such a great gift, and right at the beginning: the favour of letting us address God as our *Father*. She says: 'This favour would not be so great, Lord, if it came at the end of the prayer. But at the beginning, You fill our hands and give a reward so large that it would easily fill the intellect and thus occupy the will in such a way one would be unable to speak a word' (WP 27:1).

This favour of addressing God as *Father* is so significant for Teresa that it strikes her dumb; she is ecstatic, her intellect and will captivated by the enormity of the gift. She later exclaims: 'Oh,...

how readily should perfect contemplation come at this point!' (WP 27:1). If we truly appreciated, then, what we are saying when we address God as 'Father', we would be totally entranced and captivated – and we would be unable to go any further with saying the Our Father.

Here we see a perfect example of Teresa's teaching on the three types of prayer: that vocal prayer said *attentively* – with awareness of *whom* we are addressing and *who* we are – is mental prayer and can lead to perfect contemplation. And she writes these moving words: 'Does it seem right to you now that even though we recite these first words vocally we should fail to let our intellects understand and our hearts break in pieces at seeing such love?' (WP 27:5).[12]

The Father's Burden

Teresa holds that Jesus does not only teach us *how* to pray, but also *joins with us* in praying to the Father. In so doing, not only does Jesus make himself our 'Brother'; he also obliges God, his Father, to consider us his children. Hence, Teresa maintains, Jesus places 'no small burden' (WP 27:2) on his Father.

Why does Teresa think that being Father to us is a 'burden' to God? Because, as Father, God has to endure us, no matter what we do – he loves us with an unconditional love. Teresa was very much aware of this, as we see from this prayer to Jesus:

> in being Father He must bear with us no matter how serious the offences. If we return to Him like the prodigal son, He has to pardon us. He has to console us in our trials. He has to sustain us in the way a father like this must. For, in effect, He must be better than all the fathers in the world because in Him everything must be faultless. And after all this He must make us sharers and heirs with You. (WP 27:2)

In reflecting on all that the Father has to *be* and *do* for us as his children, Teresa pleads with Jesus: 'leave Your Father free. Don't oblige Him to do so much for a people so wretched, like myself, who will not thank You properly and there are no others who will do better' (WP 27:3).[13] We see here how seriously she takes the words we speak to God in our vocal prayer. If we call God 'Father', then we oblige him to certain ways of being and acting in relationship with us. And this also, of course, means that we oblige ourselves to strive to live as his children.

Prayer and Life

For Teresa, prayer and life are inseparable. Genuine prayer is not disembodied, but has repercussions for our lives and relationships. Authentic prayer reverberates in our lives: it forms us. And so, if we call God *our* Father, this has personal, communal and social consequences: it signifies that we are *brothers and sisters*. This leads Teresa to speak of what it means to have God as our Father in relation to the social class structure pervasive in Spain at the time – an issue that continued to be of relevance to her, even after she became a nun, for the attitudes associated with this class consciousness had crept into the monastery.

In sixteenth-century Spain, people were particularly conscious of class and status. Privilege and honour were exceptionally important issues and considerations in social interactions. This ethos was reflected in how people addressed each other (the use of titles), and behaved towards others (as with the granting of precedence, for example). Those from the highest level of society, the noble class, thought of themselves as superior and consequently demanded special treatment from those in the lower classes. In the Monastery of the Incarnation, for example, there was great inequality, even among the Sisters. There were nuns from the rich and noble classes who had servants, their own private rooms, income, and an abundance of everything – while the nuns from the lower classes were treated like servants and second-class citizens; they did not have private rooms but slept in dormitories, and at times they did not even have enough to eat.

Teresa insists: really to accept God as *our* Father means that we relinquish any kind of class distinction and reject any claim to privilege and honour. Speaking specifically to her nuns, but in words that are applicable to us all in our communal and social interactions, Teresa urges: 'Such an attitude doesn't belong here. In this house, please God, may there never be any thought about such a thing; it would be a hell. But the one who is from nobler lineage should be the one to speak least about her father. All the Sisters must be equal' (WP 27:6). Truly to recognise and acknowledge that we all have the same Father means that we must regard all people as equal, irrespective of race, sex, class, social status or any other differences.[14]

Jesus Reversing Social Structures

Teresa goes on to show that Jesus, knowing how people act with respect to class and status, reverses the structures of his society. He does this by deliberately, she feels, placing a fisherman (Peter) – from the lowest rung in society – as the head of his Church, above a king's son (Bartholomew), as she saw him[15] – from the highest rung, the nobility: 'O college of Christ, where St Peter, being a fisherman, had more authority – and the Lord wanted it so – than St Bartholomew, who was a king's son! His Majesty knew what would

37

take place in the world where people dispute over lineage' (WP 27:6).

Acknowledging God as our Father, Teresa urges us to behave as children – sons and daughters – of the *one* Father, and not to create disharmony or divisions in community by appealing to social status and its attendant claims to honour, privileges and precedence (cf. WP 27:6). She by no means exhausts her reflections on these first words of the Lord's Prayer, *Our Father*. On the contrary, she exclaims to her nuns: 'Oh, God help me! How much there is in these words to give you consolation' (WP 27:7).

Teresa encourages us to continue our own reflections on this astounding gift of having God as our Father – assuring us that the Holy Spirit, who is the bond between the Father and the Son, will unite us to them 'with a very great love' (WP 27:7).

Chapter 4
Who art in heaven

In reflecting on the words *Who art in heaven*, Teresa teaches us the *prayer of recollection*, which might also be referred to as the 'prayer of companionship' – 'holy fellowship with our Companion' (WP 29:4), as Teresa says. Recollection is a method for engaging in *mental* or *interior* prayer, which can also be practised while we are praying vocally.

A Word on 'Method'

It is well to begin with a word on 'method' or 'techniques' in prayer. For Teresa, prayer is *friendship with God*; hence, it can never be reduced to just a method or technique. We can only relate with God as we *are*, and so pray as we *can*. This is not, of course, to deny the value of techniques; they can sometimes be very helpful. But the danger is that we can forget that these are only *means* to an *end* – not 'ends' in themselves. If we lose sight of this fact, we can become focused on perfecting our method, all the while forgetting that it is only a bridge to something else: namely, encounter and relationship with God.

Generally speaking, Teresa gives *principles*, in her writings, to help us with prayer, but tends to shy away from methods. For that very reason, the fact that she *does* disclose this 'method' of prayer – recollection – is significant, so we would do well to listen to her carefully. She confesses:

> I never knew what it was to pray with satisfaction until the Lord taught me this method. And it is because I have always found so many benefits from this habit of recollection that I have enlarged so much upon it. (WP 29:7)

In encouraging us to practise this method of prayer, she says: 'Once this recollection is given by the Lord, you will not exchange it for any treasure' (WP 29:7). It is clear, then, that Teresa esteemed this way of prayer very highly.

'Heaven' and the Divine Indwelling

Teresa introduces the prayer of recollection by first reflecting on the nature of heaven: *What* is heaven? *Where* is heaven? These questions are important, because if we can find some answers to them, we will know *where* to seek God – who dwells in 'heaven' (cf. WP 28:1). Teresa affirms, in this important, encouraging statement: 'God is everywhere...; in sum, wherever God is, there is heaven' (WP 28:2). For Teresa, then, 'heaven' is not simply a place: rather, 'heaven' is *being in the presence of God.* Wherever we are present with God, *there* is heaven.

Teresa was deeply influenced by the *Confessions* of St Augustine, which played a part in her spiritual development. She refers to Augustine's testimony of how he sought God in creatures and in the beautiful things of creation – that is, in things *outside* himself – but eventually came to find God 'ultimately within himself' (WP 28:2). And so, with Augustine, Teresa acknowledges that God dwells within our soul. The important implication of this is that *heaven is within us.* Teresa expresses this in her now famous phrase: 'this little heaven of our soul, where the Maker of heaven and earth is present' (WP 28:5).

Like Augustine, Teresa confesses to having sought God outside herself, when she was ignorant of the fact that God was dwelling within her: 'I understood well that I had a soul. But what this soul deserved and who dwelt within it I did not understand because I had covered my eyes with the vanities of the world' (WP 28:11). Now, however, she rejoices in the knowledge that God dwells within her, and she is astounded by this: 'what a marvellous thing, that He who would fill a thousand worlds and many more with His grandeur would enclose Himself in something so small!' (WP 28:11).

To know this truth of the divine indwelling is *very* beneficial. Like Teresa in her youth, many people are simply unaware of it; tragically, so many live in ignorance of this great truth. With some regret she confesses: 'if I had understood as I do now that in this little palace of my soul dwelt so great a King, I would not have left Him alone so often. I would have remained with Him at times and striven more so as not to be so unclean' (WP 28:11). Knowledge of the divine indwelling, then, can deeply influence and shape our lives, centring them in God and assisting us to live more virtuously.

Showing us God Within

After Teresa discovered this truth of the divine indwelling, it is not surprising that she wanted to promote and spread this knowledge – and so draw us ever closer to God. She believes that it is precisely forgetfulness or ignorance of this fact that draws us to other attachments and distractions, and leads us away from relationship with God. And she knows that the reason he takes up his dwelling within us is because he loves us: 'In fact, since He is Lord He is free to do what He wants, and since He loves us He adapts Himself to our size' (WP 28:11).

One issue we can see Teresa addressing here is the *spatial* imagery we have of heaven, something she tries to counteract. Generally speaking, we tend to imagine heaven as a place 'way beyond us', 'high up in the sky' and so forth. But to imagine heaven in this way is automatically to think of God as *far away*. For Teresa, this faulty knowledge – that is, conceiving of God as distant from us – is one of the reasons why we fail to pray as well as we should. As she says so well: 'All the harm comes from not truly understanding that He is near, but in imagining Him as far away' (WP 29:5).[16]

Teresa wants to alert us to the fact that God is close to us – indeed, closer to us than we are to ourselves. Hence, we need never leave ourselves, so to speak, or go outside ourselves to find God; nor do we need to shout in order to speak with God (cf. WP 28:2; 29:5) – a point that Teresa makes more than once:

> Do you think it matters little for a soul with a wandering mind to understand this truth and see that there is no need to go to heaven in order to speak with one's Eternal Father or find delight in Him? Nor is there any need to shout. However softly we speak, He is near enough to hear us. Neither is there any need for wings to go to find Him. (WP 28:2)

Exploring the Prayer of Recollection

Secure in the knowledge that God dwells within a person's soul, Teresa formulates the 'prayer of recollection'.[17] And the first point to make is

43

that the 'prayer of recollection' is *not* something dependent on God alone, or a gift given only to a few: it is something *we can all do*, and work at, with God's help. This is how Teresa explains it: 'you must understand that this recollection is not something supernatural, but that it is something we can desire and achieve ourselves with the help of God – for without this help we can do nothing, not even have a good thought' (WP 29:4). She also indicates that this method of prayer is helpful for people with 'wandering minds' (WP 28:1). In other words, it is *particularly suitable for those who are prone to distractions*; it is also *helpful for those who find it difficult to use the mind or intellect in prayer.*

Firstly, though, what exactly *is* the 'prayer of recollection'? Teresa gives this most helpful definition of its essential characteristics – a definition that it would be useful to keep always in mind:

> This prayer is called 'recollection', because the soul collects its faculties together and enters within itself to be with its God. (WP 28:4)

As we can see, this method of prayer involves a *deliberate choice*, an act of will: to remove our senses from external stimuli, and to retire within ourselves so as to be with God. Or, as we shall see later, it involves 'refusing to be where the exterior senses in their distraction have gone or look in

44

that direction' (WP 28:5). Hence, it is something we *can* do and *must* do if we are to employ this way of praying. The benefits are inestimable.

The Practice of Recollection

Teresa has explained to us what recollection *is*. But what can we actually *do*, to recollect ourselves? Whilst there is no single way of practising recollection, Teresa suggests the following exercises.

– Imagine a 'Palace'

To help us recollect ourselves, Teresa proposes an imaginative exercise. She suggests that we should imagine our soul as 'an extremely rich palace, built entirely of gold and precious stones', fit for a great king who is our Father, and who is seated upon the throne of our heart (cf. WP 28:9). As we can see, Teresa knows the human soul to be a thing of great beauty and dignity, because it is the place where God dwells and where we are intimately present to him.

Then, she continues: we should also imagine that the beauty of this palace is *dependent on our life* – that is, on how well we live the virtues: 'The greater the virtues the more resplendent the jewels' (WP 28:9). This means that we have the ability to make our soul more beautiful (or less), depending on how we live our life. The more beautiful we make the palace of our soul by living the virtues, the more God will take delight in dwelling within us. This is how prayer and life can be seen as *complementary*.

– Make 'room for the Lord'

One important way of making our soul more beautiful – a place of welcome and hospitality for the Lord – is by emptying it of obstacles, such as vain attachments. In this way, the Lord is free to live and work in us:

> This fact is certain; and because it is so important, I bring it to your minds so often. He never works in the soul as He does when it is totally His without any obstacle, nor do I see how He could. He is the friend of all good order. Now, then, if we fill the palace with lowly people and trifles, how will there be room for the Lord with His court? He does enough by remaining just a little while in the midst of so much confusion. (WP 28:12)

Teresa also reminds us that the Lord respects our *freedom*: 'He doesn't force our will, He takes what we give Him'. And immediately afterwards comes this important consideration: 'He doesn't give Himself completely until we give ourselves completely' (WP 28:12).

Having this image of the soul before us,

becoming more acutely aware of the fact that we are temples of God, can help us in recollecting ourselves because we will recognise what great riches we have within us. This knowledge will prevent us from being ensnared by the vanities of the world, and from being caught up in all other distractions, too:

> I consider it impossible for us to pay so much attention to worldly things if we take the care to remember we have a Guest such as this within us, for we then see how lowly these things are next to what we possess within ourselves. (WP 28:10)

– 'Go' and 'Look'

In this same important chapter of *The Way of Perfection*, Teresa gives encouraging advice in which, as so often, she shows prayer to be attractive and spontaneous, and God to be accessible and human:

> All one need do is go into solitude and look at Him within oneself, and not turn away from so good a Guest but with great humility speak to Him as to a father. Beseech Him as you would a father; tell Him about your trials; ask Him for a remedy against them, realising that you are not worthy to be His daughter [or son]. (WP 28:2; cf. 28:3)

Recognising that God is so close to us – indeed, within us – Teresa encourages us to retire within ourselves to *be with* and to *engage with* God, as a child to its father. It is clear, from this, that the prayer of recollection is a prayer of *companionship*, a person-to-person encounter between God and ourselves.

However, Teresa's advice to 'go into solitude' and 'look at Him within oneself' is not necessarily an instruction to flee from people by going into a remote or deserted place. 'Solitude' does not necessarily mean physical isolation. For Teresa, 'solitude' refers to the *quality of our being present to God*. By the same token, being in physical isolation while thinking worldly thoughts and being inattentive to God dwelling within us is not Teresian solitude. On the other hand, we can be in the midst of a crowd of people and be totally recollected with God.

Recollection and Meditation

The practice of recollection leads Teresa to look more closely at the role of our mind or intellect in prayer. In one brief passage, she raises a number of relevant issues:

> For centred there within itself, [the soul] can think about the Passion and represent the Son and offer Him to the Father and not tire the intellect by going to look for Him on Mount

Calvary or in the garden or at the pillar.
(WP 28:4)

What is Teresa suggesting here? We note that she distinguishes between, on the one hand, thinking and representing; and on the other hand, tiring the intellect by 'going to look'. Both these activities involve use of the intellect, but in different ways.

In the *first* way – *thinking* about the Passion, *representing* the Son – the intellect is being employed to *bring to mind*, or to *make present to oneself*, the person of Christ in his Passion (which holds for any other scene of his life). The emphasis here, then, is on *presence with* and *attentiveness to* the person of Christ; it involves a 'being-with', a 'person-to-person' encounter with Christ in faith. Teresa is here drawing directly on her own experience, for this is the way she herself prayed. She writes, in the *Life*: 'This is the method of prayer I then used: since I could not reflect discursively with the intellect, I strove to represent Christ within me, and it did me greater good – in my opinion – to represent Him in those scenes where I saw Him more alone. It seemed to me that being alone and afflicted, as a person in need, He had to accept me' (L 9:4).

In the *second* way – *tiring the intellect*, *going to look* for Christ in various episodes of his life – the intellect is used in a *discursive* way. This is often referred to as 'discursive meditation'. It

49

involves a systematic reflection and point-by-point consideration of Christ in his Passion or in some other scene of his life. What we have here is an *intense* use of the intellect. Such reflections entail focusing in some detail on a particular scene or consideration of Christ's life, and asking ourselves such questions as: How did Christ feel? What was he thinking about and experiencing?

Teresa, then, is distinguishing between *recollection* and *discursive meditation*. Recollection is *not* discursive meditation. In a nutshell: discursive meditation involves an intense use of the mind; and recollection is a simple companionship with, and attentiveness to, the Lord dwelling within us (cf. L 9:4; WP 24.26). Hence, writing of the prayer of recollection, Teresa affirms how it can transform our vocal prayer:

> With this method we shall pray vocally with much calm, and any difficulty will be removed. For in the little amount of time we take to force ourselves to be close to this Lord, He will understand us as if through sign language. Thus if we are about to say the Our Father many times, He will understand us after the first. He is very fond of taking away our difficulty. Even though we may recite this prayer no more than once in an hour, we can be aware that we are with Him, of what we are asking Him, of His willingness to give to us, and how eagerly He remains with us. If we have this awareness, He

50

doesn't want us to be breaking our heads trying to speak a great deal to Him. (WP 29:6)

The essential aspect of the prayer of recollection, then, is not speaking or thinking, but a simple, loving, attentive presence to God.

The Benefits of Recollection

It will already be clear that there are great benefits from praying in this way. We can now look in detail at what these are.

– Disposing Ourselves for the Prayer of Quiet

The main benefit and gain, Teresa asserts, is that the 'divine Master comes more quickly to teach [the soul] and give it the prayer of quiet than He would through any other method it might use' (WP 28:4).[18] The prayer of recollection, then, is a very good preparation for *disposing ourselves for the grace of contemplative prayer* – the prayer of quiet. Teresa again emphasises the excellence of recollection for attaining the gift of contemplation, when she affirms:

> Those who by such a method can enclose themselves within this little heaven of our soul, where the Maker of heaven and earth is present, and grow accustomed to refusing to be where

the exterior senses in their distraction have gone or look in that direction should believe they are following an excellent path and that they will not fail to drink water from the fount; for they will journey far in a short time. (WP 28:5)

In sum: the prayer of recollection is a quick way to make progress in prayer and to journey to the Lord.[19]

– On Fire with Love

Teresa explains another benefit that comes from the prayer of recollection, in a beautiful passage conveying both warmth and intimacy:

The fire of divine love is more quickly enkindled when [people] blow a little with their intellects. Since they are close to the fire, a little spark will ignite and set everything ablaze. Because there is no impediment from outside, the soul is alone with its God; it is well prepared for this enkindling. (WP 28:8)

In short, when we are close to God, and shutting out everything 'from outside' that distracts us, little effort is required to maintain consciousness of God and a loving presence with him, once we have become used to practising this recollection. And this makes us ready to be 'set ablaze'.

What is this all about? Teresa remarks that when recollection is genuine, 'it is felt very clearly;

for it produces some effect in the soul' (WP 28:6). The effect produced is a new vision of the things of the world. We come to see material things in their proper perspective, and we value them accordingly. There is also, along with this, a new awakening to the things of the soul. This is often underlined physically, when in the prayer of recollection we pray with our eyes closed, so as to avoid seeing exterior things and to be more open to interior things.

A Worthwhile Struggle

Although Teresa encourages us to practise the prayer of recollection, she also cautions us that *it will not be without cost*: it will involve a struggle, and a disciplining of the senses, for recollection does not come easily or naturally to us. It requires effort, practice and patience. As she says wisely: 'It involves a gradual increase of self-control and an end to vain wandering from the right path; it means conquering, which is a making use of one's senses for the sake of the inner life' (WP 29:7). However, with perseverance and determination, we can become used to this method, and even quite adept at it, so that we then become recollected almost at will:

> If we make the effort, practise this recollection for some days, and get used to it, the gain will be clearly seen; we will understand, when

beginning to pray, that the bees are approaching and entering the beehive to make honey. And this recollection will be effected without our effort because the Lord has desired that, during the time the faculties are drawn inward, the soul and its will may merit to have this dominion. When the soul does no more than give a sign that it wishes to be recollected, the senses obey it and become recollected. (WP 28:7)

For Teresa, the benefits of recollection are so great that she urges us insistently to practise this method, as we see from another passage which is quoted here at length:

Therefore..., out of love for the Lord, get used to praying the Our Father with this recollection, and you will see the benefit before long. This is a manner of praying that the soul gets so quickly used to that it doesn't go astray, nor do the faculties become restless, as time will tell. I only ask that you try this method, even though it may mean some struggle; everything involves struggle before the habit is acquired. But I assure you that before long it will be a great consolation for you to know that you can find this holy Father, whom you are beseeching, within you without tiring yourself in seeking where He is. (WP 29:6)[20]

Teresa reminds us that nothing is learned or acquired without a little effort. However, with regard to the prayer of recollection, the effort and time invested are worthwhile and well rewarded, because it is a laying of the foundations and a preparation for any further, higher gifts the Lord may wish to bestow on us. Teresa is also confident that, with due diligence, this method of prayer can be acquired 'within a year, or perhaps half a year' (WP 29:8). And she urges us to this diligence: 'even in the midst of occupations,' she says, we must 'withdraw within ourselves' (WP 29:5).[21] Hence, Teresa advises:

> If you speak, strive to remember that the One with whom you are speaking is present within. If you listen, remember that you are going to hear One who is very close to you when He speaks. In sum, bear in mind that you can, if you want, avoid ever withdrawing from such good company; and be sorry that for a long time you left your Father alone, of whom you are so much in need. If you can, practise this recollection often during the day; if not, do so a few times. As you become accustomed to it you will experience the benefit, either sooner or later. (WP 29:7)

The whole purpose of the prayer of recollection is to come to a deep recognition and habitual awareness of the divine indwelling, and to delight in living with God dwelling within us.

Chapter 5
Hallowed be Your name, Your kingdom come

In her reflections on the petition *Hallowed be Your name, Your kingdom come*, Teresa speaks about the *prayer of quiet*.

Approaching God

Teresa begins her commentary on this petition by emphasising an important element of mental prayer: namely, the importance of adopting the *right attitude* before God when we approach him to make a request:

> Is there anyone, however foolish, who when he is about to ask for something from an important person doesn't think over how he should go about asking? He must find favour with this person and not seem rude. He thinks about what he should ask for and why he needs it, especially if he is asking for something significant, which is what our good Jesus teaches us to ask for. (WP 30:1)

Teresa advises, then, that before we make our request we should prepare ourselves – by considering *what* it is we are asking for, *why* we need it, and *how* to go about asking for it. Our petition, our speaking to God, should not be mindless, mechanical, or lacking in respect and courtesy. Here again, we see her insistence on mental prayer being joined to vocal prayer.

Submitting to God's Will

Teresa tells us that in giving us the Our Father, Jesus could have just said: 'Give us, Father, what is fitting for us' (WP 30:1). After all, the Father knows what we need and would still have provided for us. Indeed, this is the way Jesus prayed and lived his life. He was *totally abandoned* to the Father's will. Why, then, does Jesus give us so many petitions to make, in the Our Father? Teresa suggests two reasons for this.

The first is that, unlike Jesus, we are not so totally surrendered to the Father's will. Teresa's point is that we are often blind to what is good for us, and to what gives us life. Unlike Jesus, we do not instinctively trust God to provide what is truly good for us. We want what *we* want! And: 'If we aren't given what we want, being what we are, with this free will we have, we might not accept what the Lord gives. For although what He gives is better, we don't think we'll ever become rich,

58

since we don't at once see the money in our hand' (WP 30:2). Here, Teresa is alerting us as to how weak and 'unawakened' (WP 30:3) our faith in God really is.

The second reason is because Jesus wants us to consider carefully *what* we are asking for, and whether we *truly desire* what we request – so that 'if the Eternal Father should offer it to you, you will not scoff at it' (WP 30:3). Therefore, Teresa advises us: 'consider very carefully whether what you ask for is good for you; if it isn't, don't ask for it, but ask His Majesty to give you light' (WP 30:3).[22]

Being in God's Kingdom

We come now to an important point regarding Teresa's arrangement of the petitions of the Our Father. As seen from the title of this chapter, she does not separate *Hallowed be Your name* and *Your kingdom come*, as we ourselves are used to when reciting the Lord's Prayer, but keeps them firmly together. Why? Because, she says, we of ourselves do not know how to hallow, praise, extol and glorify God's name in a fitting manner. And so, *in order to help us hallow God's name, Jesus gives us his kingdom here on earth* (cf. WP 31:1).

Being in God's kingdom is sharing in the beatitude of those in heaven. It means being with

God in a state of peace, loving him and enjoying the blessedness of his company (cf. WP 30:5). In giving us such a lofty petition, then, Jesus wants us to experience, here on earth, a *foretaste* of his kingdom:

> As though by signs, He gives us a clear foretaste of what will be given to those He brings to His kingdom. And to those to whom He gives here below the kingdom we ask for, He gives pledges so that through these they may have great hope of going to enjoy perpetually what here on earth is given only in sips. (WP 30:6)

Teresa explains this 'foretaste' of life in the kingdom: it is given in the *prayer of quiet*.[23]

Introducing the Prayer of Quiet

In a short but inspiring statement, Teresa points out that the prayer of quiet is 'the beginning of pure contemplation' (WP 30:7). In contrast to the prayer of recollection, the prayer of quiet is 'supernatural, something we cannot procure through our own efforts' (WP 31:2; cf. 31:6). But she insists that while we cannot acquire this prayer – which is sheer gift – by our own efforts, nevertheless we can *dispose* ourselves for this prayer by praying our vocal prayer well – in this case, the Our Father – through joining it to mental prayer:

But since, as I say, I'm dealing with vocal prayer, it may seem to anyone who doesn't know about the matter that vocal prayer doesn't go with contemplation; but I know that it does. Pardon me, but I want to say this: I know there are many persons who while praying vocally…are raised by God to sublime contemplation without their striving for anything or understanding how. It's because of this that I insist so much…upon your reciting vocal prayer well. (WP 30:7)[24]

Teresa even goes on to cite the case of a woman who was actually raised to the *prayer of union* – the highest form of contemplation – through vocal prayer.[25]

Experiencing the Prayer of Quiet

Through the prayer of quiet, we will recognise that the Lord 'hears our petition', and we will be enabled truly to 'praise and hallow His name' (WP 31:1). The experience of the prayer of quiet is that of being peacefully in God's presence. And the person will know *experientially* that he or she is near to God in a way that is 'very foreign' to an understanding 'through the exterior senses' (WP 31:2).

This knowledge of being in God's presence is a different knowledge from one that we arrive at by our intellect enlightened by faith: it is something more. Teresa, of course, had first-hand experience of this, yet knew how difficult it is to explain, by virtue of its very nature. She says: 'the soul...fails to understand how it understands. But it sees it is in the kingdom, at least near the King who will give the kingdom to the soul' (WP 31:2).

This experience of being close to God is *delightful*: 'A person feels the greatest delight in his body and a great satisfaction in his soul' (WP 31:3). In fact, this experience is so delightful that the person thinks that he or she has attained the end state of blessedness: 'He feels so happy merely with being close to the fount that he is satisfied even without drinking. It doesn't seem there is anything else for him to desire' (WP 31:3). This is, however, a mistake. The prayer of quiet is only the *beginning* of the grace of contemplation:[26]

> In sum, while this prayer lasts they are so absorbed and engulfed with the satisfaction and delight they experience within themselves that they do not remember there is more to desire; they would eagerly say with St Peter: 'Lord, let us build three dwelling places here.' (WP 31:3; cf. Mt 17:4)

Characteristic of the Prayer of Quiet

Teresa points out that in the prayer of quiet, the three faculties – the will, the intellect, the memory – are *still*.[27] They are content not to be occupied or working, though 'they are not completely lost'

(WP 31:3). Indeed, any activity during this time is distasteful and most painful, given that being near the Lord and loving him is, as Teresa says, the 'one thing necessary':

> Persons in this prayer see that only this one thing is necessary, and everything else disturbs them. They don't want the body to move because it seems they would thereby lose that peace; thus they don't dare stir. It pains them to speak; in their saying 'Our Father' just once a whole hour passes. They are so close that they see they are understanding as though through signs. (WP 31:3)

However, in contrast to the prayer of union, as we shall see, what is characteristic about the prayer of quiet is that the *will* – and only the will – is totally *bound* and *captive*, engaged in loving the Lord. The *intellect* and *memory*, on the other hand, are *free*. And since these two faculties are not captive, people in this state are not totally oblivious of what is going on, but aware that something is happening: 'they can think of who it is they are near' (WP 31:3).

Moreover, given that *the will alone* is captive, the intellect and memory are a cause of pain. As Teresa points out so well: 'It happens that the soul will be in the greatest quiet and the intellect will be so distracted that it won't seem that the quiet is present in the intellect's house' (WP 31:8). This disturbance caused by the intellect is not only a nuisance but a source of considerable pain, for Teresa even confesses: 'sometimes I want to die in that I cannot cure this wandering of the intellect' (WP 31:8). The main cause of discontent in the prayer of quiet, then, is that the intellect torments the will and causes a stir (cf. WP 31:10). Teresa compares the activity of the will and intellect in the prayer of quiet to that of an unhappy couple – where husband and wife work against, rather than with, each other.[28]

What, then, are we to do with our wandering intellect? How should we control it? *Can* we? Again and again, Teresa counsels us: *Do not try* to bring the intellect into line. Why? For Teresa, prayer is *primarily* an act of the *will*; and in the prayer of quiet, the will is well occupied in loving the Lord. So, if the will lets go of its occupation in loving the Lord, and goes out to wrestle with the intellect in order to bring it into line, it will lose the nourishment that the Lord desires to give it through this grace.[29]

Towards the Prayer of Union

Teresa gives us an insight into the prayer of quiet by contrasting it with the *prayer of union*, which is the highest grace of contemplation.[30] In contrast to the prayer of quiet, in the prayer of union *all three faculties* – will, intellect, memory – are *captive*.

She uses the image of a mother breast-feeding her child, to convey further the *experiential* difference between these two forms of contemplative prayer (cf. WP 31:9.10). It is an image that she applies to both forms of prayer, but in different ways.

With regard to the *prayer of quiet*, Teresa says: 'the soul is like an infant that still nurses when at its mother's breast, and the mother without her babe's effort to suckle puts the milk in its mouth in order to give it delight' (WP 31:9). Here, the babe merely has to swallow the milk that is placed in its mouth. In a similar way, in the prayer of quiet, the will – like the babe – knowing that it is with the Lord, is absorbed in loving and being nourished by the Lord, without the help of the intellect (which, as we know, can be distracted and cause a stir). Teresa warns: 'If the will goes out to fight with the intellect so as to give a share of the experience, by drawing the intellect after itself, it cannot do so at all; it will be forced to let the milk fall from its mouth' (WP 31:9).

In the *prayer of union*, by contrast, 'the entire soul is united with God' (WP 31:10). Again applying the image of breast-feeding, but this time going beyond it, Teresa points out that in this instance the milk is somehow *placed within* the child's stomach – the child does not even have to swallow the milk. Similarly, in the prayer of union – unlike in the prayer of quiet, where the Lord 'wants [the soul] to work a little, although

65

so gently that it almost doesn't feel its effort' (WP 31:10) – the soul is nourished without any effort at all. God suspends the faculties, and with 'the joy He gives them He keeps them all occupied without their knowing or understanding how' (WP 31:10).

The Prayer of Quiet and Greater Graces

To return to the *prayer of quiet*: Teresa maintains that it is often a prelude to greater graces which the Lord wishes to bestow (cf. WP 31:11), such as the prayer of union, as we have just seen. However, if we are to receive these gifts, we must continue to be generous with the Lord and detach ourselves from everything in the world. With inevitable disappointment, she suggests the lack of generosity in people for the fact that 'there are not many more spiritual persons' (WP 31:12).

As noted earlier, being detached from the world does not necessarily mean leaving the world, but most essentially implies an *interior* detachment. One of the things that we must detach ourselves from, Teresa points out, is our *habitual* way of praying. People may have a mode of prayer that follows a particular structure and incorporates a list of prayers that they feel obliged to say; moreover, they will feel dissatisfied unless they fulfil this self-imposed obligation. Teresa asserts that when God wants to lead the person further, an attachment to a particular mode of prayer can be *detrimental* to their receiving the prayer of quiet:

> For they are so fond of speaking and reciting many vocal prayers very quickly, like one who wants to get a job done, since they oblige themselves to recite these every day, that even though, as I say, the Lord places His kingdom in their hands, they do not receive it. But with their vocal prayers they think they are doing better, and they distract themselves from the prayer of quiet. (WP 31:12)

Teresa mentions a favour sometimes granted with the prayer of quiet, in which this state lasts 'for a day or two' (WP 31:4). In this situation, people can feel disturbed; they recognise that they are not wholly themselves and not fully present in their work, because their will remains captive while their intellect and memory continue functioning. Teresa is very reassuring about this:

> This is a great favour for those to whom the Lord grants it; the active and the contemplative lives are joined. The faculties all serve the Lord together: the will is occupied in its work and contemplation without knowing how; the other two faculties serve in the work of Martha. Thus Martha and Mary walk together. (WP 31:5)

Three Important Counsels

Finally, Teresa provides three important pieces of advice for those who are experiencing the prayer of quiet.

Firstly, as those experiencing this grace recognise that they themselves are not the creators of this contentment, there is the temptation to try to hold on to the experience and make it last longer. However, this is foolish because the grace is *supernatural*. It is God's doing. How long the experience lasts, then, is at God's disposal, not ours. Teresa advises:

> The best way to hold on to this favour is to understand clearly that we can neither bring it about nor remove it; we can only receive it with gratitude, as most unworthy of it... (WP 31:6)

Secondly, it is good to find more solitude to be with the Lord and let him carry out his work in us. Hence, we ought to cease from too much activity in prayer, such as using many words. The temptation in prayer is to be productive by using the mind. Teresa, on the contrary, advises the person only to do what is sufficient to keep an awareness of God's presence:

> At most, a gentle word from time to time is sufficient, as in the case of one who blows on a candle to enkindle it again when it begins to die out. But if the candle is burning, blowing on it

will in my opinion serve no other purpose than to put it out. I say that the blowing should be gentle lest the will be distracted by the intellect busying itself with many words. (WP 31:7)

Thirdly, we need to recognise and accept the fact that the intellect cannot always be controlled and brought into line in the prayer of quiet. We should ignore the activity of the intellect and not try to engage with it; otherwise, everything will be lost:

> Thus when the will finds itself in this quiet…, it shouldn't pay any more attention to the intellect than it would to a madman. For should it want to keep the intellect near itself, it will necessarily have to be somewhat disturbed and disquieted. And in this state of prayer everything will then amount to working without any further gain but with a loss of what the Lord was giving the will without its own work. (WP 31:8)

*

As Teresa brings to a close her discussion of the prayer of quiet and of these great petitions in the Lord's Prayer, she says encouragingly: 'You are very close to the One you petition; He will not fail to hear you. And believe that herein lies the true praise and hallowing of His name' (WP 31:13).

Chapter 6
Your will be done, on earth as in heaven

Teresa begins her commentary on the petition *Your will be done, on earth as in heaven* by setting it in relation to the earlier lines of the Our Father. She points out that in the previous petition, *Hallowed be Your name, Your Kingdom come*, Jesus 'has asked, and taught us to ask, for something so highly valuable that it includes everything we can desire here below' (WP 32:1). This 'something so highly valuable' is being in God's kingdom, and Teresa links it with the experience of loving intimacy with God that is given in the supernatural gift of the prayer of quiet. And in the opening of the Lord's Prayer, *Our Father, who art in heaven*, Teresa reminds us that Jesus 'has granted us so wonderful a favour as to make us His brothers [and sisters]' (WP 32:1). Hence, we see that in the first two parts of the Our Father, we *receive* greatly from God.

Giving to God

Now, in contrast to those first few lines of the Our Father, in which we are recipients of God's favours, this *present* petition, *Your will be done, on earth as in heaven*, leads Teresa to reflect:

> let us see what [Jesus] desires us to give His Father, and how He offers this gift for us and what He asks of us. For it is right that we somehow serve Him in return for such great favours. (WP 32:1)

This petition, then, concerns not our receiving from God, but our *giving* to God.

Teresa takes the words *Your will be done* very seriously indeed. She maintains that if Jesus had not made this petition on our behalf, we would not have dared to make it of ourselves: because, she says, 'the task would seem to me impossible' (WP 32:2). In short, truly to *pray* and *mean* this petition would be far too costly and demanding for us, because what we are offering the Lord in this petition is considerable (cf. WP 32:5).

From her own personal experience, and from being a shrewd observer of human nature, Teresa remarks on the gap often found between our *words* (what we say to the Lord) and our *deeds* (how we live out the consequences of what we pledge). 'Don't,' she says, 'be like some religious who do nothing but promise; and when we don't follow through, we make an excuse saying we didn't understand what we were promising' (WP 32:5).

Resisting the Surrender of Our Will

It is often easy to promise something to another, but difficult to follow it through by living it out. And when it comes to giving our will to another, this is much harder still – in fact, the most difficult thing of all. As Teresa writes: 'to say that we abandon our will to another's will seems very easy until through experience we realise that this is the hardest thing one can do if one does it as it should be done' (WP 32:5).

In these last few words – on giving up our will 'as it should be done' – Teresa hints at the many *subtle* ways in which we rationalise what is, in effect, a choice *not* to surrender our will. She provides some examples which, although quite lengthy, are worth quoting in full:

> If we tell a rich person living in luxury that it is God's will that he be careful and use moderation at table so that others might at least have bread to eat, for they are dying of hunger, he will bring up a thousand reasons for not understanding this save in accordance with his own selfish purposes. If we tell a backbiter that it is God's will that he love his neighbour as himself, he will become impatient and no reason

73

will suffice to make him understand. We can tell a religious who has grown accustomed to freedom and comfort that he should remember his obligation to give good example and keep in mind that when he says these words they be not just words but be put into practice since he has promised them under oath; and that it is God's will that he be faithful to his vows and that he should note that if he gives scandal he is acting very contrary to them, even though he may not be breaking them entirely; and that since he has promised poverty, he should observe it without subterfuge, for this is what the Lord wills. But it is just useless to insist nowadays with some of them. (WP 33:1)

In all these ways, we end up compromising the genuine surrender of our will. So how, then, can we authentically live out this petition of doing God's will? The only possible way, Teresa shows us, is by *experiencing God's kingdom here on earth through the grace of contemplation* (cf. WP 32:2); this is given in the prayer of quiet or the prayer of union.

Two Kinds of Persons

In view of the considerable demands this petition makes on us, Teresa identifies two kinds of person who are afraid of this petition. One group comprises those 'who don't dare ask for trials from the Lord, for they suppose that in doing so they will be given them at once' (WP 32:3). The other group consists of those who 'fail to [ask for trials] out of humility, thinking they will be incapable of suffering them' (WP 32:3).

The first category refers to those who wish to avoid or bypass the cross of discipleship. Teresa challenges these people whom we might call 'resurrection Christians': 'I would like to question those who fear to ask for trials, lest these be given them at once, about what they say when they beseech the Lord to do His will in them. Perhaps they say the words just to say what everyone else is saying but not so that His will be done' (WP 32:3).

The second category refers to genuine disciples who wish to follow the Lord wholeheartedly, but who nonetheless are conscious of their weakness and frailty in living out their discipleship. Teresa is sympathetic to such people and encourages them: 'I myself hold that He, who gives these persons the love to ask for these means, which are so harsh, in order that they may show their love, will give them the capacity to suffer them' (WP 32:3).

For Teresa, really to pray this petition is to *open* ourselves to the *possibility* of accepting suffering and trials in the living out of our relationship with God. In this way, we are not seeking to avoid the cross. She explains what it is we can hope for in truly praying this petition and meaning it:

Don't fear that it means He will give you riches, or delights, or honours, or all these earthly things. His love for you is not that small, and He esteems highly what you give Him. He wants to repay you well, for He gives you His kingdom while you are still alive. (WP 32:6)

Hence, it is not a comfortable, easy or superficial life that we are asking for in this petition. Nor is this God's will for us.

God's Will

What, then, is God's will? And where do we find it? To answer this question, Teresa recalls the words which Jesus prayed to his Father in Gethsemane: 'Not my will, but yours, be done' (Lk 22:42). And she says to us:

Do you want to know how He answers those who say these words to Him sincerely? Ask His glorious Son, who said them while praying in the Garden. Since they were said with such determination and complete willingness, see if the Father's will wasn't done fully in Him through the trials, sorrows, injuries, and persecutions He suffered until His life came to an end through death on a cross. (WP 32:6)

In the person and life of Jesus – the One who prayed this petition most *sincerely* – we see what God's will is for those whom he *loves*. In the life of Jesus, then, we see both the perfect *openness of a human being to the will of God*; and the perfect *accomplishment of God's will in a human being.* Drawing lessons from the example of Jesus, Teresa now goes on to apply them to our own situation:

> For these are His gifts in this world. He gives according to the love He bears us: to those He loves more, He gives more of these gifts; to those He loves less, He gives less. And He gives according to the courage He sees in each and the love each has for His Majesty. He will see that whoever loves Him much will be able to suffer much for Him; whoever loves Him little will be capable of little. I myself hold that the measure for being able to bear a large or small cross is love. (WP 32:7)

What is Teresa saying here? Is she affirming that God's will for those he loves is to burden them with suffering? Does God *deliberately* and *gratuitously* send suffering into the lives of his loved ones? If we are suffering, is it because God loves us *more* than he loves others? We need now to reflect more closely on what these questions might mean.

Suffering and God's Will

When Teresa connects suffering with God's will, she is pointing out that those who, like Jesus, surrender themselves totally to God, and open themselves wholly to letting God's will be done in them, will *necessarily* encounter suffering. Indeed, she maintains that the suffering we experience in our lives is in direct proportion to our genuine desire *to do* God's will and *to accept* that God's will be done in and through us.

Why, though, is accepting that God's will be done in our lives associated with suffering and trials? It is because obedience to God's will – living in the way God intends us to live in this *fallen* world – will necessarily meet with resistance and reluctance from ourselves, as well as rejection and hostility from others. A few examples serve to illustrate this link between suffering and doing God's will, as we shall now see.

In the Gospels, God discloses his will to us. We are commanded, for example, *to love our enemies, to pray for those who persecute us, to turn the other cheek...* The issue here is: How do we *hear* and *live out* these commands of Jesus? Do we try to rationalise them in such a way that the real sting is taken out and the cost to ourselves removed? Or again, Jesus tells us *to give to those who ask.* When someone comes and asks us for money, what is our response? Do we give readily? Or do we try and rationalise our reluctance to part with our money by saying to ourselves that the person will only use it for ill purposes, such as drugs or alcohol? However, Jesus does not ask us to determine the motive behind a person's request prior to our giving. He simply asks us to give.

So, to live by the commands of God, to live the gospel *radically* in this world, is difficult and will involve suffering. Of course, there are many degrees by which we can do God's will and accept that God's will be done in us, depending on our generosity. This is why Teresa associates suffering with *love*. The more we love, and the more generous we are with God, the greater will be our surrender to God's will by a fuller embrace of the gospel. This will undoubtedly result in greater suffering and trials. Accordingly, as we have seen, Teresa very rightly concludes: 'I myself hold that the measure for being able to bear a large or small cross is love' (WP 32:7). The 'cross', here, can be understood as the suffering that comes from obedience to God in our discipleship of Jesus.

The Aim and Purpose of Prayer

Your will be done, on earth as in heaven. Teresa reminds us that praying this petition and living it – that is, making a wholehearted gift of ourselves to God, by a total surrender of our wills to him – is *the whole aim and purpose of genuine prayer.* Why? Because it is the *necessary condition* for the gift of perfect contemplation – the only way we can possibly drink from the fount:

Unless we give our wills entirely to the Lord so that in everything pertaining to us He might do what conforms with His will, we will never be allowed to drink from this fount. Drinking from it is perfect contemplation. (WP 32:9)

Teresa, in fact, points out how *perfect contemplation* and *total surrender to God* are two sides of the one reality. In the state of perfect contemplation, our will and God's will become one – that is, God carries out his will in us, and through us, without our creating the slightest impediment or obstacle:

In this contemplation...we don't do anything ourselves. Neither do we labour, nor do we bargain, nor is anything else necessary – because everything else is an impediment and hindrance – than to say *fiat voluntas tua*: Your will, Lord, be done in me in every way and manner that You, my Lord, want. If You want it to be done with trials, strengthen me and let them come; if with persecutions, illnesses, dishonours, and a lack of life's necessities, here I am... (WP 32:10)

Making a Virtue of Necessity

Teresa also points out very astutely that, whether we like it or not, God's will 'must be done,... and it will be done in heaven and on earth' (WP 32:4). God is not dependent on creatures to do his will; he does not need our co-operation. What God wills to do, God does. By the same token, creatures cannot prevent God from doing what he wills to do. Hence, Teresa advises her nuns to 'make a virtue of necessity' (WP 32:4). In other words, it is to our advantage and blessing (rather than to God's) if we accept willingly God's will in our life. In this way, all that happens will not be so painful.

Speaking to the Lord, Teresa acknowledges that she is comforted greatly by the fact that his will most certainly will be done in spite of ourselves. She recognises, realistically, that if the accomplishment of God's will was left solely to her, there would be no certainty of her embracing it. She also confesses that from experience of the great gain derived – which is, in one way, rather selfish – she has learnt to give her will freely to God. And so, she exclaims and urges us: 'O friends, what a great gain there is here! Oh, what a great loss there is when we do not carry out what we offer to the Lord in the Our Father!' (WP 32:4).

The Blessing of Doing God's Will

Teresa affirms the great blessing that comes when we surrender our wills to God completely. Our wholehearted gift of ourselves does nothing less than draw 'the Almighty so that He becomes one with our lowliness, transforms us into Himself, and effects a union of the Creator with the creature' (WP 32:11).

Our union with the Lord and the blessings of this union are gradual and progressive; ultimately, they depend on our generosity towards him, through the way in which we promise *Your will be done* and live out this promise. Teresa maintains:

> the more our deeds show that these are not merely polite words, all the more does the Lord bring us to Himself and raise the soul from itself and all earthly things so as to make it capable of receiving great favours, for He never finishes repaying this service in the present life. (WP 32:12)

She also gives us a glimpse into the marvels of the Lord's generosity: 'Not content with having made this soul one with Himself, He begins to find His delight in it, reveal His secrets, and rejoice that it knows what it has gained and something of what He will give it. He makes it lose these exterior senses so that nothing will occupy it. This is rapture' (WP 32:12).

So Intimate a Friendship

Teresa points out that in the *ultimate stages* of union with God and transformation of the soul, such an intimate friendship is established between God and the soul that now there is *no difference*

82

between the soul's will and God's will.[31] Her passage on the astonishing exchange of wills is both moving and inspiring:

> [God] begins to commune with the soul in so intimate a friendship that He not only gives it back its own will but gives it His. For in so great a friendship the Lord takes joy in putting the soul in command, as they say, and He does what it asks since it does His will. (WP 32:12)

In this situation, the soul is so totally captivated and sustained by God that it 'cannot do what it desires even though it may want to; nor can it give anything save what is given' (WP 32:13). Consequently, the soul suffers, because it recognises its blessings and it desires to repay the Lord in some way, yet realises its inability to do so due to its immense poverty in comparison with the greatness of God.

Teresa cautions and counsels us that we cannot possibly reach this state by our own strength or efforts; it is utterly beyond our power. Moreover, if we try to do so, we will actually spoil God's work in us. The way to reach this blessed state is to *own our poverty* and, 'with simplicity and humility, which will achieve everything' (WP 32:14), continue to pray: *Fiat voluntas tua – Your will be done.*

Chapter 7
Give us this day our daily bread

As we have seen in our discussion so far, Teresa views the Our Father not as a series of isolated petitions but as an integral whole, each request linked organically to the next. So as we move on to the request *Give us this day our daily bread*, we notice that Teresa sees it as integrally related to the previous petition, *Thy will be done, on earth as in heaven*. There she points out how difficult it is, truly to pray with sincerity and conviction that God's will be done, as this involves a radical, wholehearted gift of ourselves to God. She now explores how Jesus comes to our aid to help us make this gift of ourselves.

A Necessary Means

Accordingly, Teresa understands the petition *Give us this day our daily bread* as a *means* which Jesus adopts to help us to do God's will. She writes: 'We are weak and He is merciful. He knows that a means was necessary... He saw that doing the

Father's will was difficult' (WP 33:1). Moreover, she asserts that if the Lord had not given us this means and help, there would have been 'very few who would have carried out these words He spoke for us to the Father, *fiat voluntas tua*' (WP 33:1; cf. Mt 6:10). So, this present petition, Teresa affirms, provides us with the means to do God's will, and is at the same time an expression of Jesus' love for us in our weakness.[32]

What exactly, though, is this means or remedy of Jesus which aids us in doing God's will? It is precisely the Eucharist, which comes from what Teresa sees as Jesus' resolve 'to remain with us here below' (WP 33:2). Jesus knows, given our weakness, what a vital offering he is making on our behalf. He also knows what a difficult offering it implies for himself. And if our words are to become deeds, we need to be inspired daily by Jesus' courage and love. As Teresa points out: Jesus 'doesn't remain with us for any other reason than to help, encourage, and sustain us in doing this will that we have prayed might be done in us' (WP 34:1).

The Humility of Jesus

Teresa affirms the *humility* of Jesus in asking to remain with us: for as his will is one with the Father's, he knows that the Father would consider his every request worthy. Jesus does not, then, *need*

86

to ask the Father but, Teresa says, 'He wanted, as it were, to ask permission' (WP 33:2). Why? Because, since to remain with us 'was something so serious and important, He desired that it come from the hand of the Eternal Father' (WP 33:2).

Teresa also observes Jesus' *generous and selfless love for us* in making this request. She understands the full implications of it when she says: 'He was asking for more in this request than He was in the others' (WP 33:2). We might wonder, at first sight, what she means by 'the others'. In fact, she is referring to the other petitions of the Our Father. The words *Give us this day our daily bread* are, she says, a petition that Jesus made in his own name and in ours (cf. WP 33:1). She sees it, then, as another form of his request to remain with us: for Jesus' desire always to be with us implies the gift of the Eucharist, which in turn implies his Passion and death. This is the full import of the current petition of the Our Father.

Teresa now reflects on the great generosity of the Father and the Son in their self-giving love for us. She even remonstrates with them about this. She points out to the Father that he lets his Son give himself for us without reserve. He endures insults and rough treatment for us, which continues in his presence in the Eucharist. Here, Teresa has in mind the blasphemies and sacrileges committed against the Eucharist by the 'Lutherans'.[33] She pleads with the Father:

O eternal Lord! Why do You accept such a petition? Why do You consent to it? Don't look at His love for us, because in exchange for doing Your will perfectly, and doing it for us, He allows Himself to be crushed to pieces each day. It is for You, my Lord, to look after Him, since He will let nothing deter Him. Why must all our good come at His expense? Why does He remain silent before all and not know how to speak for Himself, but only for us? (WP 33:4)

Daily – This Day

Teresa is keenly aware that Jesus undergoes all this suffering for us silently and without self-regard. His only concern is for our good and our welfare. In this connection, Teresa highlights the fact that in this petition alone Jesus repeats the words: he asks the Father to give us this *daily* bread, and then he asks that we be given it *this day* (cf. WP 33:4). It should be noted here that in the Castilian version of the Our Father, Teresa would have prayed, 'Give us our daily bread this day' – the word order being the reverse of the English version.[34] However, these two complementary aspects – 'day' and 'daily' – are the same in both languages: the emphasis is jointly on the bread *for today*, and this bread *every day.*[35]

Teresa interprets this repetition as Jesus asking to be allowed to *serve* us each day, because he belongs to us now – until the end of the world (cf. WP 33:4; 34:1–2). She also observes that Jesus says 'our bread', which is a clear sign of his having assumed our nature and become one of us: 'Since by sharing in our nature He has become one with us here below...He says, "our bread"' (WP 33:5; cf. 33:1). In this way, Teresa points out, he identifies with us totally: 'He doesn't make any difference between Himself and us' (WP 33:5), she writes. But, Teresa contends, if we do not give ourselves each day for Jesus, then we, unlike him, *do* make such a distinction (cf. WP 33:5). This is a valuable insight and an important challenge.

Spiritual Bread

For Teresa, as we have seen, the bread referred to in this petition is the bread of the Eucharist – it is *spiritual* bread, not material bread. She is adamant that in this petition Jesus 'is teaching us to set our wills on heavenly things and to ask that we might begin enjoying Him from here below' (WP 34:2). She is concerned that 'once we start worrying about bodily needs, those of the soul will be forgotten!' (WP 34:2).[36]

We must remember that Teresa's convents were founded on poverty; therefore, the nuns relied on other people to provide them with their material needs. This meant that there was a real possibility that they *could* go hungry. Yet, Teresa insists that the nuns should *not* be anxious about this matter. With Jesus, given to us in the Eucharist, we can suffer and endure everything, she says:

> There is no need or trial or persecution that is not easy to suffer if we begin to enjoy the delight and consolation of this sacred bread. (WP 34:2)

Her counsel, not to worry about our physical sustenance, is brought out more strongly in her advice concerning times of prayer, when she insists that we must not be preoccupied with material things: 'Don't worry about the other bread, those of you who have sincerely surrendered yourselves to the will of God...; there are other times for working and for earning your bread.' Rather, she urges: 'Leave this care...to your Spouse; He will care for you always' (WP 34:4). To this end, she affirms that we must be like servants totally focused on the work in hand: that is, *prayer*, in which we should be concerned solely with pleasing our Master. Material concerns are not our business; it is the Master's responsibility to provide for us (cf. WP 34:5).

The Eucharist and Bodily Healing

Teresa links the Eucharist with bodily healing. She maintains that the Eucharist is *not only* a spiritual sustenance, but also a truly life-sustaining medicine for bodily ills as well: 'Do

90

you think this heavenly food fails to provide sustenance, even for these bodies, that it is not a great medicine even for bodily ills? I know that it is' (WP 34:6). Speaking of herself anonymously, she confesses:

> I know a person with serious illnesses, who often experiences great pain, who through this bread had them taken away as though by a gesture of the hand and was made completely well. This is a common experience, and the illnesses are very recognisable, for I don't think they could be feigned. (WP 34:6)

Faith in the Real Presence of Jesus

Teresa possesses a lively and living faith in the Real Presence of Jesus in the Eucharist. She affirms that in the Eucharist we have Jesus as *really* and *fully* present and accessible as when he was on earth. Hence, she observes that there is no *substantial* difference between Jesus' *sacramental* presence *now* (in the Eucharist) and his *physical* presence *then* (during his time on earth). The only difference is that now we behold him by faith – not by sight. And so, with regard to people who wished to have lived at the time Jesus walked this earth, she confesses that she 'wondered what more they wanted since in the most Blessed Sacrament they had Him just as truly present as He was then' (WP 34:6).

Of course, we are creatures with senses, so it is not always easy to live by faith. We desire to see, to behold, our Beloved. It is possible, then, that having Jesus under the appearances of bread and wine may temper our joy and happiness (cf. WP 34:3). Teresa addresses this issue: 'If it pains you not to see Him with your bodily eyes, consider that seeing Him so is not fitting for us' (WP 34:9). Why is it not fitting? She now shows us why.

A Divine Disguise

Teresa raises the question of why we are not permitted to see Jesus with our bodily eyes, even though people saw him with their eyes when he was on earth. She answers succinctly: 'To see Him in His glorified state is different from seeing Him as He was when He walked through this world' (WP 34:9). In other words, we are simply not capable of enduring the sight of the glorified Jesus: it would terrify us because of our sins and our unworthiness; it would make living life on earth too burdensome, since we would recognise that 'all the things we pay attention to here below are lies and jokes' (WP 34:9). Yet, for all that, he is just as close to us as he was to his closest friends when he was on earth.

We need to be aware – and with great gratitude – that by choosing to be *sacramentally* present with us, under the appearances of bread and wine,

Jesus is manifesting his humility and care for us. Teresa explains it as follows: in the Eucharist, Jesus is like a king who freely chooses to come in disguise. In this way he lets us approach him with ease, without intimidating or frightening us because of our unworthiness to be in his presence. She explains this with insight and simplicity:

> If a king were disguised it wouldn't matter to us at all if we conversed with him without so many gestures of awe and respect. It seems he would be obliged to put up with this lack since he is the one who disguised himself. Who would otherwise dare approach so unworthily, with so much lukewarmness, and with so many imperfections! (WP 34:9)

Beneath the appearances of bread and wine, then, Jesus hides his glory – so that we can all the more easily remain with him and commune with him.

Experiences of Jesus' Presence

Teresa does not rule out the possibility that Jesus can give us *palpable intimations and experiences of his presence*. But as to who receives these experiences, or as to the nature of these revelations, this is not dependent on us but on Jesus: 'He reveals Himself to those who He sees will benefit by His presence. Even though they fail to see Him with their bodily eyes, He has many methods of showing Himself to the soul, through great interior feelings and through other different ways' (WP 34:10). Teresa's only encouragement is simply to be present with Jesus and attentive to him after receiving Communion. The rest is up to him: 'Be with Him willingly; don't lose so good an occasion for conversing with Him as is the hour after having received Communion' (WP 34:10).

To this end, she strongly urges us to use *the prayer of recollection after Communion*. This practice also serves as a way of strengthening our faith in the Real Presence of Jesus in the Eucharist: 'after having received the Lord, since you have the Person Himself present, strive to close the eyes of the body and open those of the soul and look into your own heart. For I tell you, and tell you again, and would like to tell you many times that you should acquire the habit of doing this every time you receive Communion and strive to have such a conscience that you will be allowed to enjoy this blessing frequently' (WP 34:12).

Teresa again encourages the practice of the prayer of recollection when she speaks of *spiritual communion*. This is when we do not, or cannot, actually receive Communion but when we have a desire to do so: 'When you do not receive Communion...but hear Mass, you can make a spiritual communion. Spiritual communion is highly beneficial; through it you can recollect yourselves in the same way after Mass, for the love of this Lord is thereby deeply impressed on the soul. If we prepare ourselves to receive Him, He never fails to give in many ways which we do not understand' (WP 35:1).

Teresa distinguishes *being present to the Real Presence after Communion* from discursive meditation, the latter involving an intensive use of the imagination: 'Receiving Communion is not like picturing with the imagination, as when we reflect upon the Lord on the cross or in other episodes of the Passion, when we picture within ourselves how things happened to Him in the past. In Communion the event is happening now, and it is entirely true. There's no reason to go looking for Him in some other place farther away' (WP 34:8).

The Use of Pictures and Images

After Teresa points out that receiving Communion is 'not like picturing with the imagination', she elaborates further, with regard to the actual use of pictures and images as an aid to prayer. While she does not discourage this in general, she emphasises that *after Communion* is not the appropriate time for this. Why? Precisely because of Jesus' *real*, sacramental presence within us:

> If you have to pray to Him by looking at His picture, it would seem to me foolish. You would be leaving the Person Himself in order to look at

a picture of Him. Wouldn't it be silly if a person we love very much and of whom we have a portrait came to see us and we stopped speaking with him so as to carry on a conversation with the portrait? (WP 34:11)

At other times of prayer, though, Teresa recommends the use of images. Indeed, she herself loved praying before pictures of Christ and found them of great profit in nurturing her faith and nourishing her relationship with Jesus. This is what she counsels:

> Do you want to know when it is very good to have a picture of Christ and when it is a thing in which I find much delight? When He Himself is absent, or when by means of a great dryness He wants to make us feel He is absent. It is then a wonderful comfort to see an image of One whom we have so much reason to love. Wherever I turn my eyes, I would want to see His image. With what better or more pleasing thing can our eyes be occupied than with One who loves so much and who has in Himself all goods. (WP 34:11)

These two passages provide an interesting parallel: we do not need pictures or images – and should not use them – when we have the real *presence* of Christ within us. But when we experience his apparent *absence*, then they can be of great value. Teresa's teaching is both inspiring and practical.

*

Teresa concludes her commentary on the petition *Give us this day our daily bread* by urging us to persevere in the practice of recollection as we pray to Jesus within us, even though we may find it difficult or be tempted to believe that we will profit more from other methods of prayer: 'the devil will make you think you find more devotion in other things and less in this recollection after Communion' (WP 35:2). If we find ourselves thinking this, we have only to recall Teresa's words of encouragement: 'Do not abandon this practice; the Lord will see in it how much you love Him. Remember that there are few souls who accompany Him and follow Him in trials. Let us suffer something for Him; His Majesty will repay you for it' (WP 35:2).

Chapter 8
Forgive us our debts
as we forgive. . .

As with the previous petitions, Teresa situates *Forgive us our debts as we forgive those who are indebted to us* within the context of the whole of the Lord's Prayer. She points out that in the previous petition, *Give us this day our daily bread*, Jesus had asked the Father to let him stay with us in the Eucharist, in order to help us do the Father's will – for which we had prayed: *Your will be done.* Teresa shows us that, having granted us the gift of himself in the Eucharist to help us do the Father's will, Jesus then prays: 'And forgive us, Lord, our debts as we forgive our debtors' (WP 36:1).[37]

As We Forgive

The first point Teresa makes with regard to the wording of this petition is that Jesus does not say: 'as we will forgive', but: 'as we forgive' – that is, in the *present*, the here and now.[38] Teresa interprets this to mean that anyone who has received the gift of Jesus himself, and who has sincerely and truly surrendered their will to the Father, will not delay in forgiving but will do so as soon as possible (cf. WP 36:2).

Here, Teresa observes, we can see why the saints were pleased to suffer unjust wrongs and persecutions – for in praying this petition, and in forgiving those who persecuted them, they had something to offer God in return for his forgiveness of their sins. But Teresa bemoans her own poverty: because she feels that, unlike the saints, she has little or nothing to forgive others. She laments that, being the person she is, a miserable sinner, she stands more in need of *being forgiven* than of forgiving: 'What will someone as poor as I do, who has had so little to pardon and so much to be pardoned for?' (WP 36:2). And she wishes that she really did have some injury to forgive, so that she, like the saints, could offer the Lord something in exchange for his forgiveness of her sins – though we also get an encouraging glimpse, here, of her understanding of the importance and value of authentic desires:

> In sum, my Lord, I have nothing as a result to give You by means of which I may ask You to forgive my debts. May Your Son pardon me; no one has done me an injustice, and so I have nothing to pardon for your sake, unless, Lord, You accept my desire. (WP 36:2)[39]

Teresa speaks of the great exchange in this petition, whereby we receive so much for so little: 'This is a matter...,' she writes, 'that we should reflect upon very much: that something so serious and important, as that our Lord forgive us our faults,...be done by means of something so lowly as our forgiving others' (WP 36:2). And she adds: 'I have so little opportunity to offer even this lowly thing, that the Lord has to pardon me for nothing' (WP 36:2).

False Exaggerations

In the matter of forgiveness, Teresa warns against *false exaggerations* – conscious or otherwise – of the injuries others may have caused us. Here, she particularly focuses on honour and the breaking of rules of etiquette and propriety, whether in the Church or in society, which cause slights and insults to people. The reason Teresa focuses on these is because they were a great problem in her day, much more so than in our own.

In sixteenth-century Spain, society was very conscious of class and status. One could, for example, cause grave insult simply by using the wrong title when addressing someone, as people took great pride in their lineage. It was perhaps inevitable that this kind of sensitivity would have crept into monastic communities, too. Hence, Teresa pleads: 'pay no attention to the little things they call wrongs. It seems that, like children, we are making houses out of straw with these ceremonious little rules of etiquette. Oh, God help me, Sisters, if we knew what honour is and what losing honour consists in!' (WP 36:3).

The point Teresa is making is that we can easily make a fuss about nothing, simply because we don't know the nature of *true* honour. Indeed, she says that there was a time when she herself was blind to this – when she 'prized honour without understanding what it was' (WP 36:3). She confesses:

> I was following the crowd... Oh, by how many things was I offended! I am ashamed now. Yet, I wasn't at that time one of those who pay close attention to these little rules of etiquette. But neither was I careful about the main rule, because I didn't consider or pay any heed to the honour that is beneficial; that is, the honour that benefits the soul. (WP 36:3)

Teresa, then, cautions us not to deceive ourselves with the thought that we have done a great deal by forgiving a person who has slighted our honour, and so imagine that we are deserving of the Lord's forgiveness for our own sins. The fact is: we approach the Lord *empty-handed*, because what we are offended by is frequently exaggerated in our minds. So, Teresa prays: 'Help us understand, my God, that we do not know ourselves and that we come to You with empty hands; and pardon us through Your mercy' (WP 36:6).

False Honour

For Teresa, true honour consists in possessing the Christian virtues in imitation of Jesus. Attachment to worldly honours, then, is the exact antithesis of this, and contrary to spiritual growth. Naturally, Teresa decries any attachment to worldly honour in the monastery – precisely because a sense of 'honour' leads, paradoxically, to Jesus *not* being given the honour he deserves. She exclaims: 'God deliver us from monasteries where they pay attention to these ceremonious little rules. He is never much honoured in such monasteries. God help me, what great foolishness, that religious seek honour in such trifles; I am astonished!' (WP 36:3).[40]

This is, then, *false* honour. Teresa provides examples of the ridiculous state of affairs that arises in monasteries when there is attachment to false honour:

> There, people ascend and descend in rank just as in the world. Those with degrees must follow in order, according to their academic titles. Why? I don't know. The one who has managed to become professor of theology must not descend to professor of philosophy, for it is a point of honour that he must ascend and not descend.

103

Even if obedience should command, he would consider the change an affront. And there will always be someone standing by to defend him and tell him that it's an insult; then the devil at once discloses reasons why even according to God's law this thinking seems right. (WP 36:4)

Teresa then continues in an ironic, but perhaps despairing, tone: that the one who has been prioress 'must remain' ineligible for any lower office; and that there is a preoccupation about who is the senior Sister – 'for we never forget this'! Also, that it is so easy to be deluded about this that 'we even think at times,' Teresa says, '[that] we gain merit by such concern because the order commands it' (WP 36:4).

Enslaved to the Ego

This attachment to worldly honours, as Teresa shows, springs from our egocentricity or *false* self-esteem. It shows itself as a lack of humility, evident in our desire to 'ascend', as Teresa expresses it, continuing in her ironic tone of voice: 'The fact is that since we are inclined to ascend – even though we will not ascend to heaven by such an inclination – there must be no descending' (WP 36:5)!

This attitude is the exact opposite of the example of Jesus, whom we are *meant* to be emulating and following: 'O Lord, Lord! Are You our Model and

Master? Yes, indeed! Well then, what did Your honour consist of, You who honoured us? Didn't you indeed lose it in being humiliated unto death? No, Lord, but You won it for all' (WP 36:5). In Jesus, the one who divested himself of his divinity and accepted humiliation unto death, we see what true honour consists of. His example shows us convincingly that we must lose our worldly notions of honour if we are to gain *true* honour.

Freed from the Ego

Contemplative souls, Teresa points out, are freed from the ego: 'Self-esteem is far removed from these persons' (WP 36:10), she says. As such, they are freed from self-seeking or egocentricity. They are totally focused on God and on the things of God. So they even prefer and desire dishonour and suffering for God's sake, rather than to have worldly honour and rest. Moreover, she adds:

They like others to know about their sins and like to tell about them when they see themselves esteemed. The same is true in matters concerning their lineage. They already know that in the kingdom without end they will have nothing to gain from this. If they should happen to be pleased to be of good descent, it's when this would be necessary in order to serve God. When it isn't, it grieves them to be taken for more than what they are; and without any

105

grief at all but gladly they disillusion others.
(WP 36:10; cf. 36:8)

As these contemplatives have been freed from worldly attachments, they 'already know what everything is worth, they are not long delayed by a passing thing' (WP 36:9). In other words, contemplatives are not shielded from or immune to pain and hurt caused by others; but neither are they detained by these hurts or consumed by them. On the contrary, when offended they do not indulge their hurt emotions, but by means of their reason they know how to turn their trials and pains into joy, and to profit from them:

> This joy comes from their seeing that the Lord has placed in their hands something by which they will gain more graces and perpetual favours from His Majesty than they would in ten years through trials they might wish to undertake on their own... Just as others prize gold and jewels, they prize trials and desire them; they know that these latter are what will make them rich. (WP 36:9)

Forgiveness – Esteemed by God

Although Teresa acknowledges the *greatness* of the virtue of forgiveness, she is also aware of the *difficulty* we experience in exercising it. Nevertheless, it is a virtue *very much esteemed* by God, because it manifests our love for one another. Given our fallen nature, life without forgiveness would be intolerable – there would be endless conflict and no possibility of real relationships.

Teresa points out that Jesus could have suggested we practise other virtues, rather than forgiveness, in return for the Father's forgiveness of our sins. Instead, he gave priority to forgiveness. Teresa writes about this with feeling:

> how the Lord must esteem this love we have for one another! Indeed, Jesus could have put other virtues first and said: forgive us, Lord, because we do a great deal of penance or because we pray much and fast or because we have left all for You and love You very much. He didn't say forgive us because we would give up our lives for You, or, as I say, because of other possible things. But He said only, 'forgive us because we forgive.' Perhaps He said the prayer and offered it on our behalf because He knows we are so fond of this miserable honour and that to be forgiving is a virtue difficult for us to attain by ourselves but most pleasing to His Father. (WP 36:7)

Contemplation –
The Means of Forgiveness

Teresa maintains that the resolute desire to forgive any injury, no matter how grave, is found especially in *contemplatives*. It is, in fact, one of the effects and fruits of the gift of perfect contemplation. Indeed, Teresa sees the resolute desire to forgive as a sign of genuine contemplation; and she uses it as a criterion for discerning whether someone is an authentic contemplative. On the other hand, when this desire to forgive is not forthcoming, she warns: 'do not trust much in that soul's prayer' (WP 36:8).

Teresa associates the capacity to suffer wrongs, and to forgive unconditionally, with the *prayer of union* – which is the fullest gift of contemplation, the highest possible intimacy with God in this life.[41] Indeed, she insists that *forgiveness and the prayer of union go together.* One cannot exist without the other: 'the resolve to suffer wrongs and suffer them even though this may be painful… will soon be possessed by anyone who has from the Lord this favour of the prayer of union' (WP 36:11). And Teresa emphasises the point: 'If one doesn't experience these effects and come away from prayer fortified in them, one may believe that the favour was not from God but an illusion, or the devil's gift bestowed so that we might consider ourselves more honoured' (WP 36:11).

Teresa is adamant that even though true contemplatives may have other faults and imperfections, they never lack the virtue of forgiveness:

> I repeat that I know many persons whom the Lord has favoured by raising [them] to supernatural things, giving them this prayer or contemplation that was mentioned and, even though I see other faults and imperfections in them, I have never seen anyone with this one; nor do I believe that such a fault will be present if the favours are from God... (WP 36:13)

Hence, Teresa urges those who believe they are receiving the graces of contemplation to monitor themselves, as it were: to observe if they are growing in their resolve to forgive. If they find they are not, then they are *not* receiving the graces they believe God is giving them – 'For God's favour always enriches the soul it reaches' (WP 36:13).

Drawn into the Heart of God

Although this point is already compelling – that a true contemplative is able to forgive readily and with ease – Teresa realises that we need to understand *why* this is so. She explains that a contemplative – that is, a *genuine* contemplative – is, by definition, someone who comes close to the merciful God. And the effects are profound, as she explains:

> I cannot believe that a person who comes so close to Mercy itself, where he realises what he is and the great deal God has pardoned him of, would fail to pardon his offender immediately, in complete ease, and with a readiness to remain on very good terms with [that person]. (WP 36:12)

Genuine contemplatives, then, are those who have been drawn into the heart of God, have had their sins and sinfulness revealed, and have experienced God's unconditional forgiveness and mercy. It is this experience that empowers true contemplatives to extend forgiveness to others for the paltry offences committed against themselves. They see in God's light.

Chapter 9
Lead us not into temptation (1): Discerning the Temptations

Teresa moves on to the next petition, *Lead us not into temptation*, by affirming that those who pray their vocal prayers well, such as the Our Father, will be specially favoured by God and reach a high state in the spiritual life. In short, they will enjoy the graces of contemplation. She also affirms that these contemplatives, because they are so well sustained by God, have *no fear* – they are 'not afraid of anything' (WP 37:4). Indeed, they can even forget that they live in the world and are subject to attack from the *enemies* belonging to this world (cf. WP 37:4).

These enemies are a constant threat to our relationship with God and to our following of Jesus. So, Teresa cautions that we need greater self-knowledge and must not forget or lose sight of the dangers that surround us. Our fall will be from a higher place and thus all the more damaging for all concerned. This, she says, is

111

why Jesus – being 'a wise and cautious teacher who foresees the dangers' (WP 37:5) – adds the following two petitions to our prayer: *Lead us not into temptation, but deliver us from evil* (cf. WP 37:5). The first of these will be the subject of this chapter and the next.

'Soldiers of Christ'

The first point Teresa makes is that contemplatives – 'those who reach perfection' (WP 38:1) – are not afraid of trials, temptations, struggles or persecutions. She maintains: 'This is another very great and certain effect of the contemplation and the favours His Majesty gives' (WP 38:1). Such generosity and courage are indeed true signs for discerning a person's spiritual maturity. Where these signs are evident, the Lord's Spirit is truly present and there is no illusion.

Contemplatives, Teresa affirms, are not only unafraid of trials, they positively 'desire, ask for, and love trials' (WP 38:1). What does this surprising statement mean? Certainly, it does not mean masochism – that is, seeking trials and sufferings for their own sake, as an end in themselves. Rather, it means that contemplatives are not timid – they are not deterred by trials, persecutions, struggles and so on. On the contrary: they *willingly accept them* in the service of the Lord. Contemplatives are 'soldiers of Christ' (WP

38:2): they want to fight; they want to conquer, and to spend themselves for the Lord. Indeed, their willingness to endure trials and struggles is a means of proving their love for Christ.

'Public' and 'Traitorous' Enemies

These 'soldiers of Christ' are not intimidated by what Teresa refers to as 'public enemies' – that is, people, things, events in the world, *external to ourselves*. Contemplatives do not fear them because these 'public' enemies are easily recognised, and defeated with the strength the Lord provides (cf. WP 38:2).

The enemies contemplatives *do* fear, instead, are the 'traitorous enemies, the devils who transfigure themselves into angels of light, who come disguised' (WP 38:2). Teresa urges contemplatives to fear them 'and always ask the Lord to be freed from them' (WP 38:2). But who are these 'traitorous' enemies? From the examples Teresa gives, they can be seen *not only as devils but also, at least in part, as the evils that lie deep in our own spirits*: those unconscious drives and motives that are obstacles to our relationship with God.[42]

These enemies are subtle and difficult to detect; we are not readily aware of them. For this reason, we are easily deceived by them. They do us harm without our recognising their insidious, destructive presence – until it is too late. Teresa writes about this danger quite graphically: 'They suck away our blood and destroy our virtues, and we go about in the midst of the same temptation but do not know it' (WP 38:2). It is with regard to *these enemies*, Teresa maintains, that we ask the Lord, in this petition, to free and protect us. She prays:

> Eternal Father, what can we do but have recourse to You and pray that these enemies of ours not lead us into temptation? Let public enemies come, for by Your favour we will be more easily freed. But these [traitorous enemies]; who will understand them, my God? We always need to pray to You for a remedy. Instruct us, Lord, so that we may understand ourselves and be secure. (WP 39:6)

There is no doubt: we are right to fear these traitorous enemies, and we need God's special help to recognise and overcome them.

Harms Caused by Traitorous Enemies

Teresa is such an experienced guide in the spiritual life that she herself is a great help to us in learning how to overcome these traitorous enemies. She does this by helping us to *discern and recognise them* – by making us *alert to the various means by which they can cause us harm*. She provides six examples, which we will look at now. They are: false delights in prayer; false virtue; false particular virtues; false humility; excessive penances (with a false understanding of obedience); and false self-assurance. From this list, it will immediately become clear that the harms caused by the traitorous enemies are to do with *falsehood*; they are ways in which we deviate from the truth.

False Delights in Prayer

The *least effective way* in which these enemies can harm us is 'by making us suppose that the delights and consolations they can feign in us are from God' (WP 38:3). The devils, then, can mislead us by stirring up within us *feelings of consolation* in prayer. Some consolations can, of course, be from God. But, regardless of the source, the danger arises when we start to grasp at these delights in prayer and feel special, imagining them to be a *reward* from God. Whereas our prayer, in fact, could be sterile and ineffective – a mere self-indulgence.

To guard ourselves against this harm, Teresa exhorts us to *strive always for humility* – that is, for true self-knowledge – and to recognise that we are 'unworthy of these favours'. And she especially urges us: 'do not seek them' (WP 38:4). We can guard ourselves against this harm, then, through simple, faithful perseverance in our religious exercises – irrespective of how we feel or what we experience – and through not relying on consolations and delights in prayer.

Teresa praises the strength and power of humility against the devil. She contends that *humility is the best weapon in this battle*: 'I hold that the devil loses many souls who strive for this humility' (WP 38:4), she writes. She affirms that if we have genuine humility, then no matter what evils we are confronted with, the Lord will turn them to our good.

However, as mentioned, being tempted to hold on to consolations in prayer is *the least* of the temptations we may suffer. Why is this? The reason is that we can, unwittingly, use this temptation *against* the devil, insofar as such delights help us to make progress in our relationship with God:

> For, in being fed on that delight, such a person will spend more hours in prayer. Since he doesn't know that the delight is from the devil and since he sees he is unworthy of those consolations, he doesn't stop thanking God. He will feel greater obligation to serve Him and, thinking the favours come from the hand of the Lord, he will strive to dispose himself so that God will grant him more. (WP 38:3)

False (and Real) Virtue

A *more serious and effective way* that the devil brings us harm – a 'great deal of harm' – without our being aware of what is happening, is in the area of *virtue*. Teresa says plainly that what he does is 'to make us believe we have virtues when we do not' (WP 38:5). This ploy of the devil is much more subtle and insidious, as Teresa explains with great perceptiveness and nuanced understanding. For, with false consolations and delights, she says, we are aware of *receiving*, and so we feel an obligation to serve. But with regard to false virtue, it seems to us that we are *serving*, and so we feel we deserve to be rewarded.

This is, obviously, a false mentality; and the way it causes harm, Teresa says, is that it gradually weakens humility and makes us grow careless about acquiring the virtue we think we already possess. We need a remedy for this false consciousness – and it is precisely, says Teresa, this petition of 'prayer and supplication to the Eternal Father not to let us enter into temptation' (WP 38:5).

Understanding Real Virtue

To help us see more clearly the nature of false virtue, against which we need to be on our guard, Teresa explains the nature of true virtue. A genuine virtue is, *first of all*, a *gift* from the Lord.

117

Therefore, the Lord can take it back – which 'in fact often happens,' says Teresa, 'but not without His wonderful providence' (WP 38:6). When the Lord takes away the gift of his virtue, it is always for our good: that we may learn and grow spiritually. Teresa provides examples from her own life which demonstrate how she experiences virtues as gifts. Even though the following passage is long, it is worth quoting in full:

> Sometimes I think I am very detached; and as a matter of fact when put to the test, I am. At another time I will find myself so attached, and perhaps to things that the day before I would have made fun of, that I almost don't know myself. At other times I think I have great courage and that I wouldn't turn from anything of service to God; and when put to the test, I do have this courage for some things. Another day will come in which I won't find the courage in me to kill even an ant for God if in doing so I'd meet with any opposition. In like manner it seems to me that I don't care at all about things or gossip said of me; and when I'm put to the test this is at times true – indeed I am pleased about what they say. Then there come days in which one word alone distresses me, and I would want to leave the world because it seems everything is a bother to me. And I am not alone in this. I have noticed it in many persons better than I, and know that it so happens. (WP 38:6)

It is clear from this account that virtues can be given and taken away, as God sees fit, and so we can never attribute virtues to ourselves as if they belonged to us. The virtues we may think we possess are not inherently ours. We have no control of them, as Teresa says so well: 'For at the very moment when there is need of virtue one finds oneself poor' (WP 38:7). We can never be presumptuous about our virtues. We must recognise that they come from God, and that 'we do not know when the Lord will want to leave us in the prison of our misery without giving us anything' (WP 38:7).

The best and safest way to acquire and walk in virtue is by *serving the Lord with humility*, and by *cultivating a spirit of poverty*. If we always consider ourselves to be poor and without virtue, and if we wait on the Lord to provide the virtue we require, we will make ourselves secure against deception. And Teresa gives us a strong warning: 'if this poverty of spirit is not genuinely present at every step,...the Lord will abandon us' (WP 38:7). Yet even then, this is far from being the disaster it sounds. For, she adds: 'this abandonment by the Lord is one of His greatest favours, for He does it so that we might be humble and understand in truth that we have nothing we haven't received' (WP 38:7).

False Particular Virtues

Another temptation by the devil, Teresa observes, is when he deceives us into thinking that we possess a *particular* virtue, such as patience. Moreover, our experience, in some concrete instance, would appear to confirm that we do indeed possess patience. This successful instance in our exercise of the virtue can lead us to rest secure and feel satisfied, convinced that we are indeed patient.

But, Teresa counsels, we must *not* rest secure or feel satisfied: 'I advise you not to pay any attention to these virtues; let us neither think we know them other than by name nor, until we see the proof, think the Lord has given them to us' (WP 38:8). In short, Teresa cautions us to recognise that, although we may have been successful in exercising a virtue in one instance, we have not really been *fully tested* in this virtue – because it will happen that when we least expect it, we will fail in this virtue. Her point is that a virtue is not acquired easily or cheaply, nor is it acquired as a permanent possession. It will cost us much hardship if we are truly to acquire a virtue; and even then, it is only held as a *deposit* – on loan, so to speak (cf. WP 38:8).

Another example Teresa gives is with regard to poverty of spirit: 'So often do we say we have this virtue that we end up believing we have it' (WP 38:9). Yet, when put to the test, we fail: in other words, we can *delude* ourselves – falsely convince ourselves – that we have a virtue when in fact we haven't. A virtue is only really present in *act*, in *exercising* the virtue – not in imagining or thinking of the virtue.

Hence, Teresa strongly urges us to walk cautiously and without presumption. She points out that when there is a genuine solid virtue given by the Lord, 'it seems it carries all the others in its wake' and we feel the difference – 'This is something felt very clearly' (WP 38:9), she comments. The safest way to walk, then, is in humility, recognising that even though it seems we possess a virtue, we could always be mistaken. She affirms: 'The truly humble person always walks in doubt about his own virtues, and usually those he sees in his neighbours seem more certain and more valuable' (WP 38:9).

False (and True) Humility

Teresa distinguishes between two kinds of humility: *false* and *true* humility, and she adds emphasis to her argument by saying explicitly that she is speaking from personal experience. She chooses to reflect on humility because it is not easy to discern true from false humility, given that the latter can look and feel genuine: 'Consider carefully…the matter I'm going to speak to you about, for sometimes it will be through humility and virtue that you hold yourselves to be so wretched, and at other times it will be a gross temptation. I know of this because I have gone through it' (WP 39:2). We can look, now, at how she understands the differences between true and false humility.

False Humility

False humility, Teresa affirms, has its source in the devil. Fundamentally, the signs that false humility is present are an *exaggerated* sense of our sins, and consequently an *exaggerated* sense of our unworthiness before God. In short, knowledge of the gravity of our sins becomes all-consuming and dominates our consciousness: 'great disquiet is felt about the gravity of our sins' (WP 39:1), she says. This affliction can lead us to become scrupulous and dejected. It can even lead us to avoid prayer, because we feel unworthy of a relationship with God.[43]

The pain caused by false humility gives rise to *disturbance* and *agitation*; it also results in a *loss of confidence in God* (cf. WP 39:1–2). Teresa acknowledges that the situation can get so bad 'that the soul thinks God has abandoned it because of what it is; it almost doubts His mercy' (WP 39:1).

The real problem with false humility is that it is self-focused and self-centred, not God-centred.

The pain and sorrow felt with regard to our sins is not directed towards God. It is not the result of our having wounded and compromised our relationship with God. Rather, it arises from our having failed *ourselves* – from our having fallen short of our ideals and self-imposed standards.

In other words, false humility is a *subtle form of pride*. Teresa gives us some concrete advice that we should put into practice as soon as we find ourselves in this condition: 'stop thinking about your misery, insofar as possible, and turn your thoughts to the mercy of God, to how He loves us and suffered for us' (WP 39:3).

True Humility

True humility, on the other hand, also leads to pain and to recognising the seriousness and gravity of our sins. But unlike false humility, it 'does not disturb or disquiet or agitate, however great it may be; it comes with peace, delight, and calm' (WP 39:2). The pain of true humility 'expands [the soul] and enables it to serve God more' (WP 39:2).

True humility, then, in contrast to false humility, is God-centred, not self-centred. The pain, in true humility, arises from the recognition that we have fallen short and compromised our *relationship with God*. And our only concern is to learn from our faults as to how we can serve God better in the future. A sign that humility is genuine is that the person does not lose confidence in God and his mercy. People who are truly humble, then, recognise themselves as sinners who are nevertheless greatly loved by God.

Teresa reminds us that humility is the *necessary condition* in the life of prayer, for it is authentic self-knowledge. Hence she advises: 'however sublime the contemplation, let your prayer always begin and end with self-knowledge' (WP 39:5). True humility is the staple of the spiritual life; it is the bread that must be eaten with every meal.

Excessive Penances

This temptation concerns the subtle motives for doing penance. Again, as Teresa points out, the motive is *self-focused*. As she observes: we do the penance 'so that we might think we are more penitential than others and are doing something' (WP 39:3). Teresa was always sceptical of *self-imposed* penances because she had a healthy distrust of personal motives. Hence, she advises that we must always reveal any self-imposed penances to our spiritual guides, and strictly follow their counsel.

Here, she emphasises that any attempt to conceal self-imposed penances is a clear indication that they are a temptation – not a virtue: 'If you hide them from your confessor or prioress, or if when told to stop you do not do so, you are clearly undergoing a temptation' (WP 39:3). And she makes a very important – if seemingly obvious – statement: 'Strive to obey, even if this may be more painful for you, since the greatest perfection lies in obedience' (WP 39:3).

This last statement is important because of something that may seem less obvious to us: the virtue of obedience does not simply consist in doing something asked of us. Obedience, above all and fundamentally, demands that we submit our intellect and will to another (provided no sin is involved) and carry out their instruction or counsel – *even if* we do not see the value of it, agree to it, or understand the point of what is asked of us. In other words, obedience consists in *willingly* forgoing what we think is our own better, more enlightened judgment, and embracing what may be a seemingly unenlightened or inferior judgment or decision of another person. In short, authentic obedience demands that we surrender the control and management of our lives to another.[44]

False Self-Assurance

The temptation discussed here is to a false and illusory confidence that 'we will in no way return to our past faults and worldly pleasures' (WP 39:4). This self-assurance leads us to have a false estimation of ourselves, and so disposes us to be presumptuous in the situations we encounter on our spiritual journey. We make the mistake of thinking that we are more knowledgeable or stronger in virtue than we actually are; and so, we place ourselves in situations or occasions of sin where we inevitably fall. Accordingly, Teresa advises: 'Thus, however many delights and pledges of love the Lord gives you, never proceed with such self-assurance that you stop fearing lest you fall again; and be on guard against the occasions of sin' (WP 39:4).

*

Walking the Path of Prayer

Teresa affirms, in an important counsel to people of prayer, that all who pray are the particular target of the devil. She gives this stark warning: 'It's as though the devil tempts only those who take the path of prayer' (WP 39:7). Why is this? Because the devil's victory is greater and more effective, says Teresa, when one good and virtuous person falls than when thousands who are lukewarm commit 'public mistakes and sins' (WP 39:7). When a person who is nearing perfection falls, many people are surprised and the scandal caused is great. Moreover: 'the devil himself causes [people] to be surprised, for this surprise is to his advantage; he loses many souls through one who reaches perfection' (WP 39:7). This all sounds very discouraging.

However, Teresa *encourages us, all the more, to walk the path of prayer*: 'Unless it is very much due to their own fault,' she states, 'souls who practise prayer walk so much more securely' (WP 39:7).[45] They are less vulnerable to the devil than those who *do not* practise prayer. To illustrate her point, she uses the very Spanish image of the bullfight: '[People who pray] are like those in the stands watching the bull in comparison with [a person who does not pray] who is right in front of its horns' (WP 39:7). Teresa concludes her discussion so far, on the petition *Lead us not into temptation*, by affirming the security and protection that prayer provides:

Prayer is a safe road; you will be more quickly freed from temptation when close to the Lord than when far. Beseech Him and ask Him to deliver you from evil as you do so often each day in the Our Father. (WP 39:7)

Chapter 10

Lead us not into temptation (2): Embracing the Remedies

In our discussion so far of the petition *Lead us not into temptation*, we looked, in the previous chapter, at some of the temptations that we can encounter in the spiritual life. There, we saw Teresa speaking of two types of enemy that may destabilise our relationship with God: 'public enemies' – people and things in the world around us – and the especially harmful 'traitorous enemies', as she calls them: the devils that disguise themselves as angels of light, as well as the evils that lie deep within our hearts. Against these two types of enemy, Teresa now offers two *remedies* which God has given us, for protecting ourselves against these enemies' assaults (cf. WP 40:1): *love of God* and *fear of God*.[46]

Teresa refers to 'love' and 'fear' as 'two fortified castles from which one can wage war on the world and the devils' (WP 40:2). She maintains: 'Love will quicken our steps; fear will make us watch our steps to avoid falling along the way' (WP 40:1). Love, then, will drive us forward *trustingly* and *confidently* towards our Beloved; and fear will hold us back from *rashness* and *presumption* which could endanger our relationship with him.[47]

Interestingly, while discerning the presence of temptations is not always easy, it can likewise be difficult to discern the presence of love and fear, these two great virtues. Teresa is aware of this,[48] and so she provides us with signs for discernment. We can now take a closer look at these two virtues, beginning with love.

Love of God

A Presence Shining Brightly

Writing of the presence of the love of God, Teresa points out: 'If we possess love, we are certainly in the state of grace' (WP 40:2). Grace is the love of God present and active in us. So, Teresa acknowledges, we can truly love *only with the love of God in us*.

There are often clear signs that enable us to recognise the love of God in another person. In fact, given that so few possess this love perfectly, when it *is* present the signs of its presence are strongly evident: 'there are some signs,' asserts Teresa, 'that even the blind, it seems, see. They are manifest signs, though you may not want

130

to recognise them' (WP 40:2) – the word 'want' suggesting, sadly, a wilful refusal to see the light. With regard to the presence of this love, we have only to look at certain persons – their patience, compassion, integrity, impartiality, goodness, peacefulness – to recognise that they are possessed by love of God and neighbour.

Teresa also acknowledges that while there are *degrees* of love of God, a *genuine* love of God always reveals itself, even when it exists to a smaller degree. This is Teresa's helpful explanation: 'love makes itself known according to its intensity. When slight, it shows itself but slightly; when strong, it shows itself strongly. But where there is love of God, whether little or great, it is always recognised' (WP 40:3). In short, Teresa says, it is impossible to hide *genuine* love of God: 'You will not fail to recognise this love where it is present, nor do I know how it can be concealed' (WP 40:7). Just as the love between human lovers – which is a pale imitation of the divine love – is visible and cannot be hidden, so the love between a person and God is in fact *even more visible*, and more difficult to hide:

> If we love creatures here on earth, it's impossible, we are told, to hide this, and the more we do to hide it the more it is revealed... And could one conceal a love that is so strong and just that it always increases...? (WP 40:7)

This is particularly true and characteristic of contemplatives, says Teresa, for in them the love of God 'is a great fire', and so 'it cannot but shine brightly' (WP 40:4). She warns, however, that if this *love* is not strong and firmly established, then the person should walk with *fear* – that is, with a wise and humble caution. This means that in entering any situation, people 'should pray, walk with humility, and beseech the Lord not to lead them into temptation' (WP 40:4). And she adds that we should strive to know the truth, and communicate with confessors 'openly and truthfully' (WP 40:4). If we follow these cautions, Teresa tells us, then the devil's intentions will be thwarted, and 'the things by which the devil intends to cause death will cause life' (WP 40:4).

Signs of the Presence of Love of God

Teresa gives us some concrete indications to help us discern the presence of love for God. People in whom this love is present, she tells us, *love the good* – that is, they promote, praise, defend, favour, and desire the flourishing of every good thing and every good person. They *seek and love only the truth* about things and persons; this means that they do not love vanities: things without reference to God, such as riches, delights, honours, strife and envy (cf. WP 40:3). They also *love people and things in their right measure* – which means neither excessively nor defectively, because their concern is to seek 'only to please the Beloved' (WP 40:3). Teresa asserts that, to this end, such people 'go about dying [to themselves] so that their Beloved might love them, and thus they dedicate their lives to learning how they might please Him more' (WP 40:3).[49]

If we have both love and fear of God, Teresa maintains, we should 'rejoice and be at peace' (WP 40:5). She also encourages us not to be timid in our journey to God, but to walk with a certain freedom and security, trusting in God's mercy. She warns, however, that the devil will do his best to disturb our peace by setting 'a thousand false fears' before us, so that we will not enjoy God's 'wonderful blessings' (WP 40:5).

These fears caused by the devil might also be seen as some of the concrete indications that the love of God is present in us – for they are signs that our relationship with God is under attack. One such fear the devil causes is to deceive us into thinking that, since we are such miserable creatures, God cannot possibly be the source of the favours we enjoy (cf. WP 40:5–6). In this way, the devil causes two kinds of harm. The first is that he makes people afraid to engage in prayer, because they think they will be deceived. In other words, they become disturbed when they experience God's graces in prayer, as they believe that these come from the devil. The second harm is that, through this fear, he dissuades people from believing that God *does* grant favours to sinners – naturally, he does not want people to know this, because if they did they would turn to God even more ardently (cf. WP 40:6). Teresa's message is ultimately reassuring, though: that the devil 'cannot win us over' (WP 40:5). She adds, however, that he can still 'try to make us lose something' (WP 40:5). We must always be vigilant.

A Longing to Possess Love

Teresa acknowledges that 'it is a delight to speak about the love of God.' But, she asks: 'What will it be like to possess it?' (WP 41:1). Here, she is alerting us to an important distinction between 'speaking' (or thinking) and 'possessing'. Just because we are able to *speak* about spiritual realities such as prayer or love for God, this does not in fact mean that we *possess* these realities. The danger and illusion lie in the fact that we *think* we possess them if we speak about them. Teresa exclaims: 'May the Lord give [love for God] to me because of who His Majesty is' (WP 41:1).

Teresa goes on to express her great desire to possess love for God in an *exclusive* way – that is, without love for any other creature. She prays, or rather pleads: 'Let me not leave this life, O my Lord, until I no longer desire anything in it; neither let me know any love outside of You, Lord, nor let me succeed in using this term "love" for anyone else' (WP 41:1).[50] It is important to recognise that Teresa is not denigrating love of creatures. Rather, she is affirming that love of God must take precedence and priority over love of people and things, so that everything must be loved *within the context of our love for God*. The struggle we encounter comes from the fact that we can be so captivated by the beauty and goodness of creatures that we instead love God merely *within the context of our love for creatures*.

Teresa maintains that every other love – that is, love for any created thing – is ultimately, at an essential level, 'false': because 'the foundation is false, and so the edifice doesn't last' (WP 41:1). Such a love is not trustworthy, for we may love others but they may betray us. Unlike love for God, then, which is secure and which God reciprocates in full, nothing else can give us that kind of security in loving. Hence, Teresa says mockingly:

> I don't know why we are surprised. I laugh to myself when I hear it said: 'That person repaid me badly.' 'This other one doesn't love me.' What does anyone have to repay you for, or why should anyone love you? This experience will show you what the world is, for your very love for it will afterward punish you. (WP 41:1)

Teresa concludes her reflection on love for God by urging us to *pray* for it and to *do* what we can to cultivate it. Then, when death comes, we will experience security in the knowledge that 'we are going to be judged by the One whom we have loved above all things' (WP 40:8). We will experience ourselves as *going home*: 'It will not be like going to a foreign country' (WP 40:8), she says. To this end, Teresa urges us to give ourselves fully to God here on earth and to praise God, even if we have to endure sufferings. And the rewards will be great, even now: 'Even from here below you can begin to enjoy glory! You will find no fear within yourself but complete peace' (WP 40:9).

Fear of God

Fear Born of Love

By 'fear of God', Teresa does not, as mentioned, mean 'servile' fear. *Servile* fear arises from a perception or understanding of God as Someone filled with wrath and ready to punish. Rather, she means *filial* fear – the fear of a child who loves its parents and does not want to hurt them. This kind of fear, then, is born out of a *personal loving relationship* and shows itself in the care we take not to hurt or disappoint the One we love. Hence, for Teresa, fear of God does not refer to the nature or being of God, but to the nature of our relationship with him – which needs to be sensitive, respectful and loving.

Teresa tells us that the fear of God is 'easily recognised by the person who has it as well as by those who approach [that person]' (WP 41:1). So, not only do we know if we fear God, but we also could not hide this from others even if we wanted to. Teresa adds, however: 'in the beginning [fear of God] is not so developed, unless in some persons to whom…the Lord grants great favours, for in a short time He makes them rich in virtue. Hence this fear isn't discernible in everyone – at the outset, I mean. It goes on increasing in strength each day' (WP 41:1).

Signs of the Presence of Fear of God

How do we know that we have fear of God? What are the *signs*? Teresa explains that, at first, 'one starts to turn away from sin and its occasions and from bad companions' (WP 41:1). In short, we take precautions not to offend God in any way, or to compromise our relationship with him.

She also tells us that, in *contemplatives*, both fear of God and love of God are strongly manifest. Such people are *never careless* in the service of God. No matter how advantageous to their own interests something may be, they never offend against their relationship with God by putting self before God. Contemplatives 'will not advertently commit a venial sin', and 'mortal sins they fear like fire' (WP 41:1).

When urging us to cultivate the fear of God and grow in it, Teresa warns us to beware of 'illusions involving sin' (WP 41:1). This kind of illusion refers to knowingly doing or choosing what only *appears* to be good. This means that we do or choose what appears to be a good action, *objectively* speaking; but *subjectively* (in terms of our motives), the *real* reason we do this is to satisfy our selfish desires – to gratify the self. An example might be doing some penance that *appears* good or virtuous, but which is, in fact, *not* good or virtuous due to its being in conflict with the advice of our confessor or spiritual director.

As Teresa sees so well: *sin* involves a small and subtle choosing for *self*. And for a contemplative, *no* sin – not even a minor or 'venial' one – is a small matter. To appreciate her thinking, we need to investigate what we might call her 'theology of sin' – the understanding of sin that underlies Teresa's teachings.

Teresa's Understanding of Sin

First, though, we need to establish a few criteria for judging the implications and seriousness of sin. To put it simply, there are two basic approaches to an understanding of this. One is *legalistic* – whereby a sin entails breaking a *law* or contravening a *rule*. The second is *relational* – and here, a sin entails deliberately breaking or compromising a loving *relationship*, rather than a law or rule. These approaches can, of course, co-exist and are not mutually exclusive, though we often tend to emphasise one over the other.

In addition, there are three elements that determine the seriousness of a sin. The first of these is the *matter* in question: Quite simply, how grave *is* the act? (Murder, for example, being obviously more serious than gluttony.) The second is *knowledge*: Does the person know and understand what they are doing, as well as the possible repercussions for their relationship with God and others? The third is known as *deliberation* (in the sense of how the decision for the action was made): Is the person acting *freely* and *willingly*, and without coercion (from either internal constraints or external pressures)? All these elements need to be taken into account when discerning the seriousness of a sin.

Having established these criteria, we can now look at *Teresa's own understanding of sin*, and see it in a wider context. Her own 'theology of sin', so to speak, is undeniably more *relational* than legalistic: for Teresa, sin involves deliberately compromising (or even breaking) a loving relationship, rather than going against a rule or law. That is why, as mentioned above, she emphasises the issue of *deliberation* – doing something with full knowledge or awareness – when she speaks of sin: 'Be careful and attentive

– this is very important – until you see that you are strongly determined not to offend the Lord, that you would lose a thousand lives rather than commit a mortal sin, and that you are most careful not to commit venial sins – that is, advertently' (WP 41:3).

Crucially, the *matter* of the sin is not the real issue for Teresa. *Her* concern is, rather: Does this action (whether big or small) have a negative effect on my loving relationship with God? This is why, as we have just seen, she cautions us to be 'careful and attentive' (WP 41:3) – until we are so well established in the fear of God that we will not knowingly ('advertently') commit even the smallest sin, so much do we love him.

The 'Psychology of Sin'

Teresa gives an insightful description of what we might call the 'psychology of sin'. Again, underpinning everything is her *relational* understanding of sin, which leads her to focus on how *deliberate* a sin might be. She distinguishes here between sin that is *very deliberate* and sin that is *not so deliberate* (cf. WP 41:3). With regard to the first kind, she explains:

> It seems to me a sin is very deliberate when, for example, one says: 'Lord, although this grieves You, I will do it; I'm already aware that You see it, and I know You do not want it, and I

understand this; but I want to follow my whim and appetite more than Your will.' (WP 41:3)

And Teresa makes this heartfelt prayer: 'from any very deliberate sin, however small it may be, may God deliver us' (WP 41:3). She also speaks of the awareness that accompanies the less deliberate kind of sin, and observes:

> [it] comes so quickly that committing the venial sin and adverting to it happen almost together in such a way that we don't first realise what we are doing. (WP 41:3)

Teresa's *relational* understanding of sin is clear from both these degrees of sin. She sees all sin as the *deliberate* compromising or betrayal of a *loving relationship with God*, in which we make choices for *self* rather than the will of God. That is why, for Teresa, a *very deliberate* sin is *never* small – irrespective of the 'matter' itself. It is because she sees everything from the perspective of a loving relationship with God that *any act* (big or small) that deliberately goes against this love is serious: 'It doesn't seem to me possible,' she writes, 'that something like this can be called little, however light the fault; but it's serious, very serious' (WP 41:3). She does not say this to frighten us, however, but to bring us up with a start and challenge us to change our lives, so that we might fear God – and love him all the more.

Growing in Fear of God

Teresa points out that the fear of God grows in us to the extent that we 'understand the seriousness of an offence against God' (WP 41:4). And she urges us: 'reflect on this frequently in your thoughts; for it is worth our life and much more to have this virtue rooted in our souls' (WP 41:4). Until we understand this, we must either avoid or tread warily concerning any occasion, situation or relationship that does not help us come closer to God. And at the same time, she reminds us that we should do everything we can to 'bend our will' to God's will (cf. WP 41:4).

Teresa assures us that fear of God 'is easy to obtain if there is true love together with a great inner determination…not to commit an offence against God for any created thing' (WP 41:4). However, she is also realistic enough to know that our wounded nature means that we *will* fall at times, *even if* we are determined not to offend God. We should not be overly discouraged about this. Instead, this should only serve to increase our dependence on God. As Teresa affirms: 'When we are more determined we are less confident of ourselves, for confidence must be placed in God' (WP 41:4). If we are determined to avoid sin, this will alert us to how fallible and vulnerable we are. This will keep us from presumption as we live our daily lives – and it will keep us all the more trusting in God.

Blessings of the Fear of God

To grow in fear of God is to acquire a blessed fruit: that of a 'holy freedom' (WP 41:4). The effects of such freedom will be nothing less than life-changing. It will enable us to go about less 'tense and constrained' (WP 41:4). We will serve the Lord with more freedom. People and situations that formerly led us into temptation and sin will do so no longer. Our love for God will grow and grow. And not only will *we* become changed, but our *way of relating* to people and things will also be changed.

Moreover, Teresa observes, when we grow in fear of God this also influences *others*: 'If previously you played a part in contributing to their weaknesses, now by your mere presence you contribute to their restraint' (WP 41:4). She reflects on how someone who is a great servant of God 'prevents things from being said against God' *by his or her very presence* – 'without uttering a word' (WP 41:5). To think of one well-known example: we doubtless would not act in the presence of someone like Mother Teresa of Calcutta as we would in the company of a less holy person. She always mediated God so powerfully that we would have had a very real sense of being, somehow, in God's presence – and this awareness would inevitably have influenced our behaviour.

Always *relational* in her approach to God, Teresa illustrates this phenomenon by using the example of relationships between friends. When we are in the company of a friend, we are careful not to speak ill of any friend of that person, and it is just the same when we are with 'servants of God': we are careful to behave in their presence in such a way that we will not offend *their* friend – *God*. Teresa explains:

> So it is with a servant of God: his friendship with God wins him respect no matter how lowly his status, and others avoid afflicting him in a matter they so well realise would grieve him; that is, they avoid offending God in his presence. (WP 41:5)

Learning a New Way of Living

Growth requires that we *learn* as we grow. And Teresa offers us some challenging counsels, both perceptive and practical, for this new stage of our spiritual life. She advises us that, once we have grown in fear of God, we must guard against becoming *tense*: 'for if you begin to feel constrained, such a feeling will be very harmful to everything good, and at times you will end up being scrupulous and become incapable of doing anything for yourself or for others' (WP 41:5). Growth in fear of God, then, should free us from spiritual timidity – the kind of fear that

144

is scrupulous and sees sin everywhere. Authentic fear of God that is born of a loving relationship does *not* constrain us. Rather, it is *expansive* and leads to *a new-found freedom in living life, such that we attract others to God*.

Teresa maintains that any kind of *scrupulosity, piousness or repression*, however good or virtuous, *will be very evident and discouraging to others*: 'it will not bring many souls to God' (WP 41:5), she says soberly. Why is this so? Because, she explains: 'Our nature is such that this constraint is frightening and oppressive to others, and they flee from following the road that you are taking, even though they know clearly that it is the more virtuous path' (WP 41:5). Teresa warns us, then, that we can actually make virtue and discipleship look *unattractive and off-putting* to others.

Another fault or harm that comes from an attitude of repression and tenseness is 'that of judging others' (WP 41:6). Good people who are *constrained* in their relationship with God tend to *judge negatively* those who do not follow *their* particular path in journeying to God. Being constrained and tense, themselves, they see any lack of constraint in others as a fault. So, for example, 'holy joy' (WP 41:6) in another person seems to them to be dissipation; telling a good joke is seen as sinning in speech, and so on. Teresa warns very strongly against this attitude:

This constraint is a very dangerous thing; it means going about in continual temptation and it bears ill effects; it is detrimental to your neighbour. To think that if all do not proceed as you do, in this constrained way, they are not proceeding well is extremely wrong. (WP 41:6)

Another harm she notices in those who are tense and constrained is that of being *overly cautious in dealing with others*:

in some things of which you must speak, and it is right that you speak, you don't dare do so for fear of going to extremes; rather, perhaps, you speak well of something that it would be very good for you to abhor. (WP 41:6)

Here, Teresa is urging us to be people of *integrity and authenticity* who *trust in God* and *speak the truth* with confidence and courage.

Teresa also invites us to make our way of life attractive to others, in order to draw them to God:

strive as much as you can, without offence to God, to be affable and understanding in such a way that everyone you talk to will love your conversation and desire your manner of living and acting, and not be frightened and intimidated by virtue. (WP 41:7)

She encourages us to be *the kind of people others love to be with* and *find easy to approach and converse with*, knowing they will *not be judged*, and not feeling constrained or intimidated in our presence; the kind of people others *wish to emulate*. In other words, we are called to *set others free to be themselves.* In a now-famous passage, Teresa makes this important observation with regard to living in community:

> This is very important for religious; the holier they are the more sociable they are with their Sisters. (WP 41:7)

This observation is applicable to *all of us*, regardless of our situation in life. As Teresa knew well from community life, it is easier to be charming and sociable with people we *don't* have to live with; the real test of holiness is how we relate to those people with whom we *do* live and work each day. It is in the *daily grind of life* that *the authenticity of virtue* is disclosed.

The Importance of Relationships

Teresa emphasises how important relationships are for spiritual growth. She writes:

> Don't let your soul withdraw into a corner, for instead of obtaining sanctity you will obtain many imperfections that the devil in other ways will place before you; and...you will not be of as much benefit to yourself or to others as you could have been. (WP 41:8)

True holiness, Teresa tells us, is not arrived at by isolating ourselves from others. We learn about ourselves – including our virtues and vices – through our relationships with others. In this way, we grow in self-knowledge through the *exercise* of virtue. In isolation, however, we can become the devil's playground – fantasising about unreality and imagining we are more virtuous than we really are; this can all too easily lead us to become judgmental, smug, self-righteous, and so on.

To attain the right kind of 'fear of God', which does not constrain but liberates us in our relationship with God and others, we must have a *right understanding of God*. Teresa says reassuringly:

> strive to think rightly about God, for He doesn't look at trifles as much as you think, and don't lose your courage or allow your soul to be constrained, for many blessings could be lost. (WP 41:8)

Teresa's God, then, is not a nit-picker! He is not someone who is constantly trying to find fault in us. If we think of God as a celestial policeman – rather than a loving father – we will keep our distance from God and lose out on the blessings of intimacy with him. The important thing, she advises us, is this: 'Have the right intention, a resolute will...not to offend God' (WP 41:8).

*

Teresa concludes her discussion by saying: 'with these two virtues – love and fear of God – you can advance on this road calmly and quietly, but not carelessly since fear must always take the lead. As long as we live, we will never have complete security; that would be a great danger' (WP 41:9).

These two virtues are what we ask for when we pray: *Lead us not into temptation.* Yes, 'fear will make us watch our steps' and 'love will quicken our steps' (cf. WP 40:1). They are the help and the compass which we can, and must, use on our journey to God.

Chapter 11
But deliver us from evil. Amen.

With considerable empathy and immersion in the Gospels, Teresa makes a claim that might at first surprise most people: that Jesus was right to *include himself* in this final petition of the Our Father: *Deliver us from evil*. Recalling these words of Jesus on the eve of his death, 'I have greatly desired to eat this supper with you' (Lk 22:15), she comments: 'Here we see how weary He must have been of living' (WP 42:1). She senses how much he would surely have longed to return to his Father, where he would be free from so many trials and evils.[51]

The Sufferings of Jesus

Teresa observes that Jesus' *whole life* was a continual death, and she has good reason for saying this: because he always *knew in advance* about his impending Passion; he lived continually with the knowledge of the terrible ordeal he was to undergo. However, Teresa senses that this ordeal

151

was not the worst of his sufferings: Jesus suffered even more because, with his great charity and the tenderness of his love for God and people, he had to witness the 'many offences committed against His Father' and the 'multitude of souls that were lost' (WP 42:1).

By contrast, she says, 'people don't tire of living even if they go on to be a hundred, but always want to live longer' (WP 42:1). Teresa attributes this to the fact that our lives are not burdened by as many sufferings and evils as was Jesus' life on earth. She does feel, though, that anyone who 'possesses charity here on earth' (WP 42:1) shares, at least to some degree, Jesus' 'torment' of knowing of souls being lost and offences being committed against the Father.

Towards Eternity

Teresa now comments on the final word of the Our Father: *Amen*, which she sees as pointing to the fact that all things on earth come to an end. And it is a word that looks forward: towards eternity. With this *Amen*, she says, Jesus is asking 'that we be freed from all evil forever' (WP 42:2).

While we live this earthly life, it is of course impossible for us, as Teresa says, to be free of 'many temptations and imperfections and even sins' (WP 42:2). And we can add to these burdens

152

the many kinds of bodily ailments and hardships from which we all suffer. Yet with regard to these, Teresa makes the important point that, although they burden us, it is nonetheless '[not] good that we ask to be without them' (WP 42:2).[52] What can this possibly mean?

Here, it should be noted that Teresa's statement does not imply neglecting our health or refusing medical help. Rather, she would appear to be speaking about ailments and burdens *from which no human remedy is able to free us*. In this sense, she would wish that, instead of rebelling inwardly against them, we might see the spiritual opportunity they offer us. She was very much aware that hardships and sufferings can have a salutary effect on ourselves and a positive influence on the Church and the world. Generally speaking, it is sufferings and hardships that make us turn to God; and uniting our sufferings to Christ – to his continuing work of salvation – lends them an unparalleled transforming power.

Set Free to Live

If it is impossible to be freed from all evils, whether bodily or spiritual, then from *what* are we asking to be freed when we pray: *Deliver us from evil?* Teresa acknowledges that the evils from which we would wish to be liberated are *particular to each individual*. For herself, she confesses:

I see myself closed in by weakness, lukewarmness, and a lack of mortification, and many other things. I see that it behoves me to ask the Lord for a remedy. (WP 42:2)[53]

Teresa finds herself hostage to these imperfections in life, and so she prays to the Lord: 'deliver me now from all evil' and 'be pleased to bring me to the place where all blessings are' (WP 42:2). For true lovers of God, there is not much in this life to hold them here, as she expresses so well in this prayer to Jesus:

What do they still hope for here, those to whom You have given knowledge of what the world is, and those who have a living faith concerning what the Eternal Father has kept for them? (WP 42:2)

Teresa would rather be set free from this life than live with the imperfections and sins that keep her from God. And with this in mind, we can now look more closely at the importance for Teresa of having *desire for God*.

Desire for God

There is no doubt that, on one level, Teresa is writing as someone who at times had a great sense of weariness, for her own life contained numerous sufferings and hardships. But at the centre of everything is her *heart full of love for God*. This informs her underlying disposition and concern, which we see in this passage: 'what is unendurable, Lord, is not to know for certain that I love You or that my desires are acceptable before You' (WP 42:2). Behind this outburst, as it were, clearly lies the fear of being deceived about her motivations – which is a possibility for all of us, due to our fallen nature: Do we love God for himself, or do we love ourselves in God?

Teresa goes on to assure us that if we ask to be delivered from the trials and evils of this life – that is, from all that keeps us away from God – 'with great desire and complete determination', then this is 'a clear sign...that the favours [we] receive in prayer are from God' (WP 42:3). And if we find ourselves doing this, we should 'esteem [our] prayer highly' (WP 42:3).

While this passage can apply to all of us, Teresa is speaking here of contemplatives in particular. She maintains that it is natural that anyone who has already tasted the consolations and blessings of God, although 'in mere sips' (WP 42:3), and has begun to enjoy his kingdom here below would desire to be with God in his kingdom. Hence, it is not so much weariness of life as *the experience of God's favours* that can make life here below seem difficult and possibly *almost unendurable*. After a direct experience of God, everything that contemplatives see here below 'will be completely dark to them' (WP 42:3).

While some might call Teresa's view of the human condition 'pessimistic', it is perhaps more accurate to describe it as 'realistic'. Teresa was clear-sighted and honest in the area of self-knowledge. She knew that we are so deeply wounded by sin that we struggle to correspond fully to the will of God. This is why she can see death as a liberation from this 'body of death', and it is in this positive light that we should understand her wish to be set free from this life:

> Oh, how different this life would have to be in order for one not to desire death! How our will deviates in its inclination from that which is the will of God. He wants us to love truth; we love the lie. He wants us to desire the eternal; we, here below, lean towards what comes to an end. He wants us to desire sublime and great things; we, here below, desire base and earthly things. He would want us to desire only what is secure; we, here below, love the dubious. Everything is a mockery...except beseeching God to free us from these dangers forever and draw us at last away from every evil. (WP 42:4)

When true lovers of God prefer death to life, and find life itself a great trial, it is because they know they cannot love God as perfectly as they desire.

Teresa is no doubt aware that she is bold in suggesting that we ask God to set us free from this life. But she still invites us to make this request –

after which we must simply wait, leaving the rest to God: 'let us leave the giving to His will since we have already given Him our own' (WP 42:4). In other words, even though the Lord will be glad that we desire to enjoy life with him in eternity, he will not grant it to us yet, nor must we wish we could hasten the moment. *Only God* can decide the right moment of our passing from this world to the next. It is the will of God that counts, and this is Teresa's dearest wish for her own life, which she sums up in the words of the Our Father:

His name be forever hallowed in heaven and on earth, and may His will be always done in me. Amen. (WP 42:4)

Epilogue

'I say we should all try to be contemplatives' (WP 18:3). To be a contemplative – and so enjoy the deepest possible intimacy with God in this life – is the goal that Teresa sets before us. She urges us to strive for this goal, and it is to this end that she provides us with her commentary on the Our Father.

In our secular world today, many people are hungering for something more, even if they cannot pinpoint exactly *what* is giving them a sense that 'something is missing', as we say. What, in fact, they are hungering for – and this 'something' is the longing of *every* human heart – is direct experience of contact with the transcendent and the divine.

Here, Teresa's reflections on the Our Father and her teachings on prayer can be most beneficial. Compared with our tendency for complicated prayer techniques, Teresa's *catechism of prayer* – as we have called her commentary on the Our Father – is a model of simplicity, requiring nothing other than a sincere desire to pray and to deepen our intimacy with God.

When Teresa concludes her commentary, she gives us a kind of afterword in which she explains what it was that she set out to do in her discussion of the Lord's Prayer. It was, quite simply, to teach and encourage us to 'pray vocally with perfection' (WP 42:4)[54] – reciting the Our Father ('vocal prayer') with our heart and mind fully engaged ('mental prayer'), so that our words are imbued with the three basic elements essential to all true prayer: to be aware of and understand 'whom you are asking', 'who it is that is asking', and 'what you are asking for' (WP 42:4). That is, having a full and vibrant focus on: *God – me – the intentions, thoughts, emotions I lay before him.*

Teresa had the highest esteem for this evangelical prayer taught by the Lord himself. She refers to the Our Father as a prayer of 'sublime perfection' in which 'everything about contemplation and perfection is included…from the beginning stages to mental prayer, to the prayer of quiet, and to that of union' (WP 37:1). And once more taking an overall glance at the Lord's Prayer, this time just after she has finished discussing its final petition, she exclaims with surprise and awe at the marvellous riches contained within the Our Father:

> Certainly, it never entered my mind that this prayer contained so many deep secrets; for now you have seen the entire spiritual way contained in it, from the beginning stages until God engulfs the soul and gives it to drink abundantly from the fount of living water, which He said was to be found at the end of the way. (WP 42:5)

Teresa points out that the Lord's Prayer is adaptable to every person and need. So, no matter who we are, or at what stage we may be in the spiritual life, we can pray the Our Father in a way that is exactly right for us. Indeed, Teresa maintains that Jesus deliberately left this prayer in an 'obscure form' (WP 37:2), so that each person can petition according to his or her own intentions and needs.

Contemplatives, as well as people who are very much committed to God, will pray the Our Father in a way that is different from people who have other needs and concerns. The first group, Teresa observes, are more concerned with spiritual goods, whereas the second are still very much earth-bound.[55] Here, it must be emphasised that Teresa is not being elitist: she is by no means denigrating those who are not contemplatives. She herself affirms that contemplation is *sheer gift* – and not our achievement – but she does suggest that we can, and must, prepare ourselves to receive this grace if the Lord, in his mercy, wishes to grant it to us.

No matter how spiritual and contemplative Teresa was herself, she understood fully the need to petition for material things, as she explains here:

Those who still live on earth, and it is good that they live in conformity with their state in life, may ask also for bread. They must be sustained and must sustain their households.

Such a petition is very just and holy, and so also is their petition for other things according to their needs. (WP 37:2)

This reveals just how realistic, practical and grounded Teresa is, in her doctrine on prayer. She acknowledges three basic premises: *prayer is for life* – life is not for prayer; *we can only pray from where we are* – not from where we may wish to be; *and we must never forget that we are human beings* – not angels. Hence, we must be attentive not only to our spiritual needs but also to our physical and material needs.

As mentioned, Teresa is astounded by the richness of the Lord's Prayer. If we truly appreciate this prayer, she says, then 'we need to study no other book than this one' (WP 37:1). It is the foundation of all authentic prayer, and a rich form of 'doctrine' as well as 'consolation' (WP 42:5). Two aspects of this 'doctrine' are so vital that they must always be practised by everyone: *giving God our will* and *forgiving others* (cf. WP 37:3). But with her great understanding of human nature, and the awareness that we are all on a journey, Teresa acknowledges that there are *degrees* as to how each of us will live out these petitions: 'The perfect will give their will in the way perfect souls do and forgive with that perfection that was mentioned' (WP 37:3). The important thing is that we *do what we can* – because 'the Lord receives everything' (WP 37:3).

What is crucial about this prayer is that it was given to us by Jesus: 'the mouth of Truth itself, who cannot err' (WP 42:5).[56] Likewise, what is crucial about *praying* this prayer, Teresa reminds us, is *sincerity* and *truthfulness*. We must be determined to *do* in our life what we *say* to God in prayer. Our deeds should correspond to our words:

> [The Lord] likes us to be truthful with Him. If we speak plainly and clearly so that we don't say one thing and then act differently, He always gives more than what we ask of Him. (WP 37:4)

For Teresa, then, prayer is a relationship with God founded on sincerity and truth. All true prayer – in line with the Lord's Prayer – is life-transforming, because it gradually unites our will with God's will. If we are sincere and truthful with God, then he himself will reward us abundantly.

We must never pray merely with our lips: rather, we must pray from the depths of our heart and with the commitment of our will, surrendering ourselves to God's action within us. In this way, we *will* be disposing ourselves for the gift of contemplation, should the Lord in his mercy desire to grant it to us. And thus we will be united with the One who gave us the Our Father.

Abbreviations and Editions Used

The translation and paragraph numbering used in this book for the writings of St Teresa are taken from: *The Collected Works of St. Teresa of Avila*, 3 vols., trs. Kieran Kavanaugh, OCD & Otilio Rodriguez, OCD, Washington, DC: ICS Publications, 1987, 1980 & 1985.

The following abbreviations are used in referring to her works:

L   *The Book of Her Life*
WP   *The Way of Perfection*
IC   *The Interior Castle*
F   *The Book of Her Foundations*
ST   *Spiritual Testimonies*

In referencing, different sections of a work are divided by a colon, and instances from the same section by a full stop. Hence, 'WP 1:3' denotes chapter 1, paragraph 3 of *The Way of Perfection*, and 'WP 1.3' indicates chapters 1 and 3.

Notes

1. From the Office of Readings, Tuesday of Week 29, in *The Divine Office*, vol. III, London & Glasgow: Collins, 1974, pp. 669–70.

2. *The Way of Perfection* can be found in Kieran Kavanaugh, OCD & Otilio Rodriguez, OCD (trs.), *The Collected Works of St. Teresa of Avila*, vol. 2, Washington, DC: ICS Publications, 1980. Note that Teresa's first manuscript of this work was written in about 1566; and her second, final, one is considered to have been completed at the end of 1566 or the beginning of 1567: see Tomás Alvarez, OCD, *St. Teresa of Avila: 100 Themes on Her Life and Work*, Washington, DC: ICS Publications, 2011, pp. 313–4. These two versions are known as the 'Escorial' and 'Valladolid' manuscripts respectively.

3. St Teresa was the first woman to be declared a Doctor of the Church: by Pope Paul VI on September 27, 1970.

4. See Kieran Kavanaugh, OCD & Otilio Rodriguez, OCD (trs.), *The Collected Works of St. Teresa of Avila*, vol. 1, Washington, DC: ICS Publications, 1987, p. 23 (from the Introduction by Fr Kieran Kavanaugh to *The Book of Her Life*). Teresa, together with Francisco de Osuna and

Bernardino de Laredo, belonged to the *recogidos*. See the discussions outlined in note 6 below.

5. See *ibid.*, p. 23.

6. For a good outline of these two movements, see J Mary Luti, *Teresa of Avila's Way*, Collegeville, MN: The Liturgical Press – 'A Michael Glazier Book' ('The Way of the Christan Mystics' series, vol. 13), 1991, p. 25. Luti refers to the two groups by the names *espirituales* (or *experimentados*) and *alumbrados* respectively. See also Rowan Williams, *Teresa of Avila*, London & New York: Continuum, 1991, pp. 28–30.

7. Teresa herself fell into this trap, with regard to reflection on the humanity of Christ, during her early years as a religious. She later came to regret this greatly, and strongly exhorted her Carmelite Sisters never to abandon this practice, no matter what stage they were at on the spiritual journey. See especially L 22 and IC VI:7.

8. See *The Collected Works of St. Teresa of Avila*, vol. 1, *op. cit.*, pp. 23–4.

9. See *The Collected Works of St. Teresa of Avila*, vol. 2, *op. cit.*, p. 22.

10. The words 'without their striving for anything or understanding how' are from Teresa's first manuscript of *The Way of Perfection*, the 'Escorial'.

11. *The Living Flame of Love* 3:36, in Kieran Kavanaugh, OCD & Otilio Rodriguez, OCD (trs.), *The Collected Works of Saint John of the*

Cross, Washington, DC: ICS Publications, 1991. John of the Cross also underlines receiving in contemplation as an active 'occupation': '[the soul's] sole occupation now is to receive from God,... it wills and consents to [the divine movements]': in *The Living Flame of Love* 1:9.

12. This brings to mind an episode in the life of St Thérèse. One day, her sister Céline found her lost in contemplation and visibly moved. Thérèse replied, with tears in her eyes, what a wonderful thing it was 'to call God our Father', and she explained that she was 'meditating on the *Our Father*': see Sister Geneviève of the Holy Face (Céline Martin), *My Sister St. Thérèse*, Rockford, IL: Tan Books, 1997, p. 109.

13. The words 'and there are no others who will do better' are from the Escorial manuscript.

14. This concern with class and status was such a sensitive issue in the monastery that Teresa strongly advises: 'When this concern about lineage is noticed in a Sister, apply a remedy at once and let her fear lest she be Judas among the apostles. Give her penances until she understands that she doesn't deserve to be thought of as made from even a very wretched kind of mud' (WP 27:6).

15. It is not known where Teresa read that Bartholomew was a king's son. It could have been from the name itself, *Bar-tholomaeus* (literally, 'son of Ptolemaeus'), or she could have read it in the *Flos Sanctorum* ('*Flower of the Saints*'): see

The Collected Works of St. Teresa of Avila, vol. 2, *op. cit.*, p. 470, note 7 (re WP 27).

16. This quotation is from the Escorial manuscript.

17. Teresa was influenced by Francisco de Osuna's book *The Third Spiritual Alphabet*, in her formulation of the prayer of recollection. In L 4:7, she speaks of the impact of Osuna's work in teaching her 'how to proceed in prayer' and 'how to be recollected'. Teresa's prayer of recollection, however, is not simply identical with that taught by Osuna: see E Allison Peers, *Studies of the Spanish Mystics*, vol. 1, London: The Sheldon Press, 1927, pp. 93–100.

18. The 'prayer of quiet', to which Teresa refers here, is a supernatural form of prayer which she presents in her reflection on the petition *Hallowed be Your name, Your kingdom come*, as we will see in the next chapter.

19. In the passage just quoted, Teresa uses the comparison of a person travelling by sea as distinct from someone travelling by land. We need to remember that in her day, unlike our own, it was quicker to travel by sea. Hence, she says of those who practise recollection: 'Their situation is like that of a person who travels by ship; with a little wind he reaches the end of his journey in a few days' (WP 28:5).

20. This entire passage is from the Escorial manuscript.

21. This is the full passage: 'We must, then,

disengage ourselves from everything so as to approach God interiorly and even in the midst of occupations withdraw within ourselves. Although it may be for only a moment that I remember I have that Company within myself, doing so is very beneficial. In sum, we must get used to delighting in the fact that it isn't necessary to shout in order to speak to Him, for His Majesty will give the experience that He is present' (WP 29:5).

22. Teresa explains: 'I am reflecting here on what we are asking for when we ask for this kingdom, and it is good that we understand our request... I want to tell you here...what I understand so that we may know what we are asking for and the importance of our begging persistently for it, and do as much as we can so as to please the One who is to give it to us' (WP 30:4).

23. 'In [the prayer of quiet] it seems the Lord... begins now to give us His kingdom here below so that we may truly praise and hallow His name and strive that all persons do so' (WP 31:1).

24. The words 'without their striving' up to 'vocal prayer well' inclusive are from the Escorial manuscript.

25. Teresa comments: 'If this account is true, as it is, those of you who are the enemies of contemplatives should not think that you are free from being a contemplative if you recite your vocal prayers as they should be recited, with a pure conscience' (WP 30:7).

171

26. It should be mentioned at this point that there is another term used by Teresa, which can also indicate another stage, that marks the beginning of contemplation. This is the prayer of (passive) recollection, not discussed in *The Way of Perfection* where 'recollection', as seen in the previous chapter, refers to an active gathering together of one's faculties (cf. WP 28–29). Teresa sometimes uses the term 'recollection' (when speaking of passive recollection) indiscriminately with the 'prayer of quiet', to denote the first degree of infused prayer (cf. L 14–15); at other times, though, she uses it to refer to the first faint experience of mystical prayer that *prepares the way* for the prayer of quiet (cf. ST 59:3). For this note I am indebted to *The Collected Works of St. Teresa of Avila*, vol. 2, *op. cit.*, p. 489, note 1 (re IC IV:3).

27. The 'intellect', here, refers to the thinking mind, or the understanding, without any overtones of 'being an intellectual'.

28. 'It's a wonderful thing when all three faculties are in accord. It's like what happens between two married people: if they love each other, the one wants what the other wants. But if the husband is unhappily married, it's easy to see what disturbance he'll cause his wife' (WP 31:8).

29. 'In this prayer the will is the ruler and the powerful one. It will draw the intellect after itself without your being disturbed. And if the

will should desire to draw the intellect by force of arms, the strength it has against the intellect will be lost. This strength comes from eating and receiving that divine food. And neither the will nor the intellect will gain anything, but both will lose' (WP 31:10).

30. The 'prayer of union' should not necessarily be seen as one stage of prayer, even though it may be called, as here, 'the highest grace of contemplation'. One Teresian scholar, commenting on the last three dwelling places of *The Interior Castle*, refers to them as a 'phase of union'. Note, too, that in addition to the mystical union of prayer, experienced in the depths of one's soul, union with God, as Teresa's writings show, also entails conformity of our will with God's will. On both points, see Alvarez, *St. Teresa of Avila*, *op. cit.*, p. 352. The prayer of union will be discussed in the next chapter.

31. Readers wishing to explore Teresa's most mature insights into the stages of union are referred to the fifth, sixth and seventh dwelling places of *The Interior Castle*, in *The Collected Works of St. Teresa of Avila*, vol. 2, *op. cit.* See also this description of an experience of mystical union: 'God so places Himself in the interior of that soul that when it returns to itself it can in no way doubt that it was in God and God was in it' (IC V:1:9).

32. 'Now then, once Jesus saw the need, He

sought out a wonderful means by which to show the extreme of His love for us, and in His own name and in that of His brothers He made the following petition: "Give us this day, Lord, our daily bread"' (WP 33:1).

33. Cf. WP 33:3; also 35:3.4. Note that Teresa refers to all Protestants as 'Lutherans'.

34. See *The Collected Works of St. Teresa of Avila*, vol. 2, *op. cit.*, p. 472, note 4 (re WP 33).

35. That is, the bread for the *whole day's needs*, which we ask for *each day*. For this latter phrase, Luke has 'each day' (Lk 11:3), and Matthew has 'today' / 'this day' (Mt 6:11) which does, though, still imply making the prayer each day. As will be mentioned, Teresa sees the words 'day' and 'daily', here, in the timeless sense of eternity (cf. WP 34:1–2) – as with the notion of the 'eternal day'.

36. These last two quotations are from the Escorial manuscript.

37. This is the version used in the translation of Teresa's works, followed here, though in the liturgy we are more familiar with the translation 'trespasses' and 'trespass'. Note that Matthew has: 'forgive us our debts, as we have forgiven [our debtors]' (Mt 6:12), and that Luke has: 'forgive us our sins, for we ourselves forgive [our debtors]' (Lk 11:4 – *Revised Standard Version* / 11:3–4 – *The Jerusalem Bible*).

38. We might also say: *in the past* (as in Matthew's version: 'forgive us our debts, *as we*

174

have forgiven...'). However, the point is the same: the *concrete action* of forgiving, and not merely a good but unrealised intention.

39. A quotation from the Escorial manuscript.

40. From the Escorial manuscript.

41. On the prayer of union, see the discussion in Chapter 6, as well as note 26 above.

42. In the remainder of this discussion, traitorous enemies will be referred to in terms of the devil or devils, in keeping with Teresa's own explanation, although in some cases, as here, the evils that lie hidden in our hearts may also be a possible interpretation.

43. Teresa herself avoided prayer for years, because she felt her sins barred her from coming worthily into God's presence. Later on, she confessed that it was one of the biggest mistakes she ever made. And she urges people *never* to give up prayer or contact with God – no matter how grave they think their sins may be.

44. This scenario is especially relevant to religious life, and needs to be counterbalanced – as it generally is today, more so than in the past – by enlightened authority and respect for the person under obedience.

45. This quotation and the next two are taken from the Escorial manuscript.

46. The phrase 'love of God' refers, in this discussion, to *our* love of God (and is sometimes expressed in this chapter as 'love for God'), while

'fear' is not to be confused with anxiety or servile fear but denotes the fear of God that is a virtue and a gift of the Holy Spirit.

47. Teresa writes: 'On this way there are many stumbling blocks for all of us who are alive and continue our journey. With this fear we will be secure against being deceived' (WP 40:1).

48. 'You will ask me how you can tell if you have these two virtues which are so great; and you are right in doing so, for you cannot be very certain and definite about them' (WP 40:2).

49. Teresa gives the examples of St Paul and St Mary Magdalene: 'Within three days the one began to realise that he was sick with love; that was St Paul. The Magdalene knew from the first day; and how well she knew!' (WP 40:3).

50. This quotation and the next one are from the Escorial manuscript, as is the indented quotation from WP 41:1 below.

51. The word 'evils', here, should be understood not just as the onslaughts of the evil one, but also as sufferings, hardships and other burdens.

52. These two quotations are from the Escorial manuscript.

53. This passage is from her first manuscript, the 'Escorial'. Here, Teresa also poured out, in a heartfelt way, a list of things from which she wished to be freed: 'Deliver me, Lord, from this shadow of death, deliver me from so many trials, deliver me from so many sufferings, deliver me from so

many changes, from so many compliments that we are forced to receive while still living, from so many, many, many things that tire and weary me, that would tire anyone reading this if I mentioned them all' (WP 42:2). Note also that in this final chapter of *The Way of Perfection*, Teresa removed a number of 'Escorial' passages from her final version. As before, these are indicated in notes as and when they are quoted.

54. The passages quoted in this paragraph are from the Escorial manuscript.

55. 'Contemplatives and persons already very much committed to God, who no longer desire earthly things, ask for the heavenly favours that can, through God's goodness, be given on earth' (WP 37:2).

56. This quotation is from the Escorial manuscript.

TERESIAN PRESS
SOME FORTHCOMING PUBLICATIONS

Living with God: St Teresa's Understanding of Prayer
Tomás Álvarez, OCD

*Journey of Love: Teresa of Avila's Interior Castle
– A Reader's Guide*
Eugene McCaffrey, OCD

A Moment of Prayer – A Life of Prayer
Conrad De Meester, OCD

St Paul: A Gospel of Prayer
James McCaffrey, OCD

What Carmel Means to Me
Edited by James McCaffrey, OCD & Joanne Mosley

*Captive Flames: A Biblical Reading of
the Carmelite Saints* – **to be reissued**
James McCaffrey, OCD

Teresian Press
Carmelite Priory
Boars Hill
Oxford OX1 5HB

www.carmelitebooks.com

MOUNT CARMEL

A REVIEW OF THE SPIRITUAL LIFE

The flagship magazine of the Teresian Carmelites
of Great Britain and Ireland

OUR AIMS

To help people in every aspect of their lives by sharing and exploring with them the rich sources of Carmelite teaching on prayer, within the broad perspective of Christian spirituality and life experience.

Articles, poems and book reviews

We publish contributions by Carmelites and non-Carmelites alike

Some comments by our readers:

"As good as a book – wonderful for sharing the faith."
(A missionary sister in Nigeria)

"What a helpful magazine.
I always look forward to receiving my copy."
(A lay reader in Australia)

"It helps me write my homilies
and sustains me during prayer."
(A parish priest in the United States)

"Ideal for busy people: great spiritual depth
but in article length."
(A spiritual director in Ireland)

If you would like a free sample copy, please contact:

Mount Carmel / Teresian Press
Carmelite Priory
Boars Hill
Oxford OX1 5HB
England
www.carmelitebooks.com